Generis
PUBLISHING

AF410081

THE DISTINCTIVENESS OF THE CATHOLIC PRIESTHOOD IN A RELIGIO-PLURALISTIC GHANA

Leo Andoh Korsah

CIP a Camerei Naționale a Cărții

Korsah, Leo Andoh. The distinctiveness of the catholic priesthood in a religio-pluralistic Ghana / Leo Andoh Korsah. – Chişinău : Generis Publishing, 2020 (Print on demand). – 73 p. Bibliogr.: p. 66-69. – Referinţe bibliogr. în subsol.

ISBN 978-9975-154-46-8.

272/273(667) K 74

Cover image: www.pixabay.com

Generis Publishing
Online orders: www.generis-publishing.com
Orders by email: info@generis-publishing.com

DEDICATION

To the mysterious "King Melchizedek of Salem, Priest of the Most High God" (Heb 7:1, Gen 14:18), also to all priests of blessed memory, present and future priests of the Most High God.

FOREWORD

Religious pluralism naturally implies the existence of plurality of religious leaders due to the perceived religious functions and roles they perform in both private and public worship. Such religious pluralism has directly and indirectly occasioned the emergence of multiform of pastors, seers, evangelists, apostles, priests and diverse men of God in Africa especially Anglophone West Africa. This phenomenon seems to pose a huge challenge and a big question to the nature and distinctiveness of priesthood in the Catholic Church.

This book, a bold scientific reflection from a lay catholic, is an attempt to addressing the issue of the distinctiveness of the Catholic priesthood amidst religious pluralistic society like Ghana. The author, Leo Ando Korsah from religious perspective, demonstrates with clarity the pluralistic nature of the Ghanaian society. From his analysis, he articulates theologically by emphasizing on the distinctiveness of nature of the Catholic Priest and recommends that it should not be confused with other religious leaders/diverse men of God. The author elucidates his arguments from the biblical, historical and theological perspective.

To underscore the distinctiveness of Catholic priesthood he at the same time studied the nature of the priesthood from other traditions such as, African Traditional Religion; Protestant Traditions (Presbyterian Church of Ghana and Methodist Church, Ghana); and African Indigenous Church (Musama Disco Christo Church).

Leo Andoh Korsah employs simple and clear language to communicate for all to understand, although this is a well-researched scholarly work for all who desire to broaden their knowledge on the Priesthood.

I have known Leo since his postgraduate studies at the Department of Religious Studies at the Kwame Nkrumah University of Science and Technology, Kumasi, Ghana, and his writings are reflections of the kind of student he was.

I recommend this book to the lecturer, students, priests, seminarians and the laity.

Rev. Fr. Francis Kwame Appiah-Kubi, PhD
(Senior Lecturer)
Department of Religious Studies, KNUST.
Kumasi, Ghana
October, 2020.

TABLE OF CONTENTS

LIST OF ABBREVIATIONS

AA	Apostolicam Actuositatem
AICs	African Indigenous/Initiated/Independent Churches
MDCC	Musama Disco Christo Church
NRSV	New Revised Standard Version
OT	Optatam Totius
PDV	Pastores Dabo Vobis
PO	Presbyterorum Ordinis
RH	Redemptoris Hominis
SC	Sacrosanctum Concilium
SO	Standing Order

CHAPTER I

INTRODUCTION TO RELIGIOUS PLURALISM IN GHANA

1.0. Introduction

In almost, if not all religions, there may be a distinct person chosen to lead worship. In a religiously pluralistic society like Ghana, there is the need to know and understand the specific roles of such people in their various religions in order to avoid confusion and know the appropriate terms to use for them. In this book, we seek to elucidate the distinctiveness of the Catholic priesthood in the midst of Ghana's religious pluralism. In this introductory chapter we commence the discussion with the religious plurality of the Ghanaian society, with references to brief historical overview of the three main religions.

1.1.0. Religious Pluralism in Ghana

Religious pluralism is acknowledging, accepting and respecting the existence and uniqueness of other religions without sharing in their faith. Ghana is religiously pluralistic; made up of three main religions and these are African Traditional religions, Christianity and Islam. Greater number of the Ghanaian population professes Christianity (71.2%), followed by Islam (17.6%), a minority but significant of the population adhere to African Traditional religions (5.2%) while another minority (5.3%) are not affiliated to any religion.[1] In terms of those who profess religion, adherents of the African traditional religions are in the minority although both Christianity and Islam are not indigenous to Ghanaians. These two religions were introduced into the country by the Christian and Muslim missionaries respectively.

We shall delve briefly into religious pluralism in the Ghanaian society with references to the historical overview of the three main religions. There are over one hundred (100) ethnic groups in Ghana and these groups have not only maintained their ethnic identity[2] but also religious identity. The various ethnic groups have something distinct about their traditional religion which makes it particular to that ethnic group. The distinctions and particularities of what is practiced by the various

---

[1] Ghana Statistical Service, *2010 Population & Housing Census Summary Report of Final Results.* 2012. Pg 6.

[2] Microsoft, "Ghana". In: *Microsoft Student 2009 [DVD].* Redmond, WA: Microsoft Corporation, 2008.

ethnic groups make it possible to argue for African Traditional Religions as some African scholars have espoused. The existence of the distinctions in African primal religions further emphasizes the assertion that "Traditional religions are not universal: they are tribal or national. Each religion is bound and limited to the people among whom it has evolved"[3].

African Traditional religions are not foreign to the Ghanaian society. They are primal and the only religions in the country until the advent of the Christian and later Islamic missionaries. The worldview of the primal religions may be divided into the spiritual and the physical. The spiritual consists of the Supreme Being, spirits (benevolent and malevolent) and the ancestors while the physical consists of the human beings, animals, trees and other inanimate objects. In the African society both the spiritual and the physical relate harmoniously to maintain a stabled society. For instance, the dead matters to the African, they are part of the society and are remembered and consulted whenever necessary. J.S. Mbiti elucidates that in African Traditional religion there is no formal distinction between the spiritual and physical because the religion is part of the African life. The African does not separate the sacred from the secular; the two are always intermarried and this is seen in activities such as sowing and harvesting of crops or at parties or funerals[4]. Mbiti's elucidation is also applicable to the traditional religion in Ghana. Although African Traditional Religion has the minority adherents as compared to the other religions, it is very accommodative and has permeated Islam and Christianity with some of its practices.

1.1.1. Brief Historical Overview of Christianity in Ghana

Agbeti dates back the genesis of Christianity in Ghana, then Gold Coast to 1482 with the arrival of the merchants and explorers from Portugal at the Coast, to be specific Elmina in the central region[5]. The Portuguese merchants and explorers being Catholics, on their arrival mounted a cross and an altar and celebrated the first Mass. During this period, Christianity was limited only to the merchants, explorers and their crew. The Christian presence on the land was not intensive until the arrival of the Basel missionaries in 1828 who begun active and sustained Christian activities.

Scholars including Samwini who attempt giving a historical account of Christianity in Ghana observe that the first Basel missionaries served as chaplains to the Danish

---

[3] Mbiti, J.S. *African Religions & Philosophy*. London: Heinemann, 1969. Pg 4

[4] Mbiti, J.S. 1969. Pg 2.

[5] Agbeti, J.W. *West African Church History: Christian Missions and Church Foundations 1482-1919*. Leiden: E.J. Brill, 1986. Pg 3.

merchants who inhabited the Christiansburg castle[6]. There was a fall out between the chaplains and the merchants because the former insisted that chaplains should concentrate on their chaplaincy works without interference into their merchandise. A chaplain, Andreas Riis, then left the castle for Akropong in 1835 where he established the first inland mission station. He established a second one by 1847 with the help of West Indian missionaries - David Rochester with Mrs. Rochester and Joseph Mohr.

The Wesleyan Missionary Society arrived in the Gold Coast (now Ghana) in the year 1835 as a response to the invitation by a "Bible Band" under the leadership of William de Graft and George Blankson[7]. These leaders requested for missionaries as well as copies of the Bible through the British governor of the Gold Coast. The Rev Joseph Dunwell, together with the Methodist Mission Society volunteered to come and they arrived in 1835. By March of the same year, fifty indigenous people became registered members of the Methodist Society. The Rev Joseph Dunwell died in the same year of his arrival. Other Wesleyan missionaries came to continue what Dunwell had started. The Wesleyan Mission persevered in spite of the problems such as the high mortality rate and it was out of this mission that the Methodist Church Ghana was established. A District Synod under the authority of the Methodist Church of Great Britain administered the Church until she attained autonomy on 28th July 1961 as the result of her "signing of the Deed of Foundation of the Methodist Church" at Cape Coast[8].

The Bremen Mission is a north German Missionary Society. Samwini dates their arrival in the Gold Coast to March 1847 under the leadership of Rev Lorenz Wolf with three other missionaries. The Bremen Mission commenced mission work at Peki among the Ewe community at the southeast of the Volta River. According to him, the Bremen missionaries also faced the old problem of high mortality rate. It is alleged that by November of the same year the other three missionaries had died. Wolf also went back to Hamburg as a result of sickness for treatment, and died on his arrival in 1851. The missionaries halted and left the Gold Coast in 1851 only to return in 1853 under the new leadership of Plessing and Dauble. On their second arrival, they went to the coastal town of Keta where they established a station[9].

---

[6] Samwini, N.I. *The Muslim Resurgence in Ghana since 1950 and its Effect upon Muslims and Muslim-Christian Relations.* Berlin: LIT Verlag, 2006. Pg 44.

[7] Agbeti, J.W. 1986. Pg 55.

[8] The Methodist Church Ghana. *The Constitution and Standing Orders of the Methodist Church Ghana.* Accra: The Conference of the Methodist Church Ghana, 2000. S.O. 2 (1).

[9] Samwini, N.I. 2006. Pg 48.

fter the 1482 Catholic enterprise of the Portuguese, again from 1572-1576 "six (6) ortuguese missionaries of the Order of St Augustine evangelized Elmina, Komenda, futu and Abura. They set up a monastery and the confraternity of St Nicholas of olentine in Elmina"[10]. Five of these missionaries lost their lives through martyrdom. he Roman Catholic Church officially sent out missionaries to the Gold Coast pecifically Elmina[11] in 1880 for proper missionary activities. These missionaries ere priests who belonged to the congregation of the Society of African Mission .M.A). By 1896 they had opened a station in Kumasi and by 1906 had opened ission stations in the north were Islam had already been established.

ut of nationalistic feelings, the African Methodist Episcopal Zion was started at ape Coast and Keta in 1898. There were also other Protestant missions that had egun missionary work in the Gold Coast and these include the Seventh Day dventist Church and the Baptist Church who both began in 1898 at Sekondi and ape Coast respectively. The Society for the Propagation of the Gospel was in ekondi by 1904; the Salvation Army at Agona Duakwa in 1911 and the Assemblies f God at Yendi in 1935[12].

y 1913 some indigenous people also established their own churches and these ecame known as the African Independent/Indigenous/Initiated churches (AICs). The frican Indigenous[13] Churches refer to churches founded in Africa by Africans and rimarily for Africans. The purpose of the AICs is to proclaim the Gospel of Jesus hrist and interpret the Gospel to suit the African situation and worldview. Scholars uch as Arnold Turner have used the term African Indigenous Churches in describing hurches that contextualize the Gospel to suit the African conception of God through er beliefs and practices. Examples of the AICs are the Church of the Twelve postles[14], Apostles Revelation Society (ARS)[15], and the Musama Disco Christo

---

[10] Cape Coast Archdiocese. 2003. *Landmarks in the history of the Catholic Church in the rchdiocese of Cape Coast, Ghana.* In: Program brochure for the Reception and Thanksgiving lass of H.E. Peter Cardinal Kodwo Appiah Turkson. Pg 13

[11] Elmina is the first place in the Gold Coast to have a taste of Catholicism. It experienced the atholic faith in 1482. 1880 was the second advent of Catholicism in Elmina and at this time round the missionaries were purposely sent for evangelistic mission.

[12] Samwini, N.I. 2006. Pg 54.

[13] The "indigenous" can be substituted with initiated, independent or instituted. The implication is hat such churches could be referred to as African Initiated/Indigenous/Independent/Instituted hurches. For the purpose of this study, we would opt for Indigenous rather than nitiated/Independent/Instituted.

[14] It was founded by Grace Tani, John Nackabah and John Hackman

[15] The ARS was founded by Mr Charles Kobla Nutonuti Wovenu who was generally known as rophet Wovenu.

Church MDCC[16]. We shall briefly look at the historical overview of the MDCC, as i
is one of the few, if not the only AIC, that recognizes ministerial priesthood.

1.1.1.2. Musama Disco Christo Church (MDCC)

The MDCC was started as a prayer group called *Egyidifu Kuw*[17] within the loca
congregation of the Methodist Church at Gomoa Oguan in 1919 in the Centra
Region. It was under the leadership of the then Catechist of the Methodist Church by
name Joseph William Egyanka Appiah who became known as Prophet Jemisemiham
Jehu-Appiah, *Akaboha I*. The MDCC came into existence after the expulsion of the
then Catechist Appiah from the Methodist Church by the Rev Gaddiel Acquaah, the
then Circuit Superintendent Minister in 1922. His expulsion was due to some beliefs
and practices that were alien to Methodism but were held up by Appiah and the
prayer group[18].

According to Baeta, the Rev Acquaah referred to such practices as occult and
cautioned "Methodists were not like that" and ordered Appiah to desist from those
practices. His failure to adhere to the order led to his expulsion from the Methodist
Church[19]. Members of the prayer group who sympathized with him also followed
him. The prayer group was then transformed into the Musama Disco Christo Church
(Army of the Cross of Christ Church) on 19th October 1922[20].

Prior to the arrival of Rev Aquaah and the expulsion of Catechist Appiah from the
church, the latter had been accused of practicing "curious magical rites and customs,
and indulging in the use of secret medicine and special drugs obtained from India and
America"[21]. The Rev Assan (who was later replaced by Rev Aquaah) investigated the
matter but did not realize any truth in the accusation and therefore could not take any
disciplinary action against Appiah.

The organizational structure of the MDCC is a blend of elements of African culture
(mostly Akan) with Christian heritage. The Prophet Appiah laid down a succession

---

[16] The MDCC was also founded by Joseph William Egyanka Appiah who became Prophet
Jemisemiham Jehu-Appiah.

[17] It means Faith Society

[18] 2009. *Mussama Church: History of MDCC* [online] (2009) available at:
http://mdccgh.blogspot.com [assessed on July 13, 2012]

[19] Baeta, C.G., Prophetism in Ghana. London: SCM Press Ltd, 1962. Pg 33

[20] 2009. *Mussama Church: History of MDCC* [online] (2009) available at:
http://mdccgh.blogspot.com [assessed on July 13, 2012]

[21] Baeta, C.G., 1962. Pg 28

plan in the form of a dynasty, which he became its precursor with the title *Akaboha I*. The *Akaboha* is regarded as a paramount chief of a state with *Nana* as his royal title and resides in a holy royal town called *Mazano* (my town). The *Akaboha* has his own elders, linguists and other functionaries of an Akan traditional royal home. He also created the office of the *Akatitibi* for the wife of the *Akaboha*. In every respect, the *Akatitibi* functions as a queen mother exercising her responsibilities in the context of African Christianity[22].

In terms of doctrines and practices, Baeta argues that the Musama Church emphasizes the equal authority of the Old and New Testaments and argues for the practice of polygamy, ritual purification and sacrifices by appealing to the Old Testament, especially Leviticus. The church has her own version of the Apostle's Creed by replacing the section with "Catholic Church" with "Musama Disco Christo Church and all true Christian churches everywhere in the world"[23].

The Musama church also believes in the existence of good angels who work for the welfare of humankind and bad angels or demons who constantly work against humankind. The church also emphasizes a strong belief in divine healing. There is the custom of *kanedua* (lamp-post) which suggests "the priesthood of each head of a household". This custom entails the head of a house fixing a lamp-post in the middle of the compound, and when it is done, it becomes a necessary requirement for the head to gather the entire household around the lamp-post with a lit lamp and lead evening prayers daily. Baeta, again emphasizes that aside these priestly functions, there are other priestly functions which are strictly reserved for the ministerial priests and the ultimate of all the priestly functions is solely reserved for the *Akaboha* whose office is also that of a High Priest[24].

Classical Pentecostalism and Neo-Pentecostalism also became another strand of Christianity in Ghana. The current church development in Ghana is the Neo-Prophetic Movements. These movements are independent neo-Pentecostal churches who emphasize on prophecies and healings and deliverances. These churches exhibit some characteristics of the AICs. We now shift our focus to the advent of Islam in Ghana.

---

[22] Ekem, JDK. 2009. Pg 122

[23] Baeta, C.G., 1962. Pg 40

[24] Baeta, C.G., 1962. Pg 45

1.1.2. Brief Historical Overview of Islam in Ghana

Islam entered into the Gold Coast through the north mostly through the activities of invaders, traders and clerics. Yim traces the advent of Islam to the northern part of modern Ghana to the 14th century, "when the Sudanic kingdoms began to grow in political and economical [sic] power because of the traders".[25] By the middle of the 1500s, Gonja in the Gold Coast had experienced some Islam; one of the traditions claims that some Bambara warriors from Niger conquered the original inhabitants in the Gonja region and established the current Gonja state even though by then some Muslims had already arrived from Begho, Hausaland and Borno.[26] The Dagomba and Wala welcomed Islam gradually. By the 17th century Islam was being practiced in Dagomba although it did not manifest any significant impact until 1700[27]. In the northern areas, Islam was integrated into the life and culture of the people.

The people of the south did not show much interest in Islam; rather they were interested in the benefits that Islam came along with. For instance, the Asante were interested in the prayers and amulets that could aid them win wars and also give them protection from their enemies. Samwini cites Levtzion that "the Asante king and his sub chiefs applied for the same supernatural aid that Muslims used to offer to their chiefs in the north, and so through the nineteenth century Asante chiefs used to invite Muslims from the north to pray for them"[28]. Islam was not integrated into the life and culture of the southern people as a result of their attitude towards the religion. The Asante and the other southern parts of the Gold Coast did not experience much Islam until the 18th century. The Ghanaian population is made up of various strands of Islam and these include: the Tijaniyya, the Ahmadiyya Mission, Ahlus Sunna wal-Jama'a. The Tijaniyya group of Muslims forms the majority of all the Islamic groups in Ghana. Islam is presently an active force to reckon with in Ghana.

1.1.3. Conclusion

The discussion so far has been on the religious plurality of the Ghanaian society. It has been established that there is religious pluralism even within the recognized religions. This is seen in the different traditional religious practices, different

---

[25] Yim, Cherlsoon. *Understanding Islam, its history in Ghana, and an effective evangelistic strategy to overcome Islamic influence in Ghana.* 2004. Doctor of Ministry thesis submitted to Liberty Baptist Theological Seminary. Lynchberg, Virginia. Pg 76.

[26] Yim, Cherlsoon. 2004. Pg 79

[27] Yim, Cherlsoon. 2004. Pg 84

[28] Samwini, N.I. 2006. Pg 32.

Christian denominations and the various strands of Islam practiced in Ghana. All the three various religions practiced in Ghana have someone who leads their worship or deals directly with the object of worship on behalf of all the other adherents of the religions. In the case of African Traditional Religion there may be several religious leaders and those who deal directly with the deity may be mediators and also preside over ritual sacrifices when necessary. Such people are referred to as African traditional priests because of their priestly functions[29]. Islam also has religious leaders such as an Imam who leads in the offering of worship and even slaughters a ram to offer sacrifice during Eid ul-Adha. Although this act of offering sacrifice may be priestly, Islam does not recognize any notion of priesthood and does not interpret this function of the Imam as priestly.

In Christianity just like the other two religions, there are those who lead worship and even in some cases serve as mediating servants. Almost, if not all the denominations have people whose duty it is to make the presence of God real in their communities of faith "through the performance of sacramental, preaching, teaching and pastoral functions"[30]. Such people may be referred to as Pastors, Prophets, Apostles, and Priests etc. depending on the particular tradition and denomination. In the next chapter the focus of the study is extensively based on the Catholic Priesthood.

---

[29] Opoku, K.A. *West African Traditional Religion*. Accra: FEP International Private Limited, 1978. Pg 74.

[30] Ekem, J.D.K. *Priesthood in Context: A study of Priesthood in some Christian and Primal Communities of Ghana and its Relevance for Mother-Tongue Biblical Interpretation*. Accra: SonLife Press, 2009. Pg 101

CHAPTER II

THE CATHOLIC PRIESTHOOD

2.0. Introduction

In the introductory chapter, we realized the religious pluralistic nature of the Ghanaian society. We also noted that all the various religious groups or denominations have specific people who lead worship or play very vital and specific role in worship. Such persons are priests in the realistic sense of the word in reference to Catholicism. Who then is the Catholic priest and how distinct is he from others. In answering this question, we shall look at the etymology of the term "priest" and focus on the Catholic priesthood; with particular attention to its historical development, theology and vocations. We shall as well delve into the formation of the candidates to the priesthood, the rites of ordination to the priesthood and the life and ministry of the Catholic priest.

2.1. Etymology of the term "Priest"

From various sources, the word "priest" is derived from the French *prêtre* and the Greek πρεσβύτερος (*presbyteros*). The word in Greek was however translated into English as "elder". The term was mostly used in the late antiquity to refer to the elders of the Jewish and Christian communities. In the course of Christian application of the term, "the semantics of the term shifted from the ordained person's place in ecclesiastical polity to his role as a cultic celebrant"[31] The Latin and Greek word for priest as a "cultic celebrant" is *sacerdos* and ἱερεύς (*hiereus*) respectively. These words emphasize religious connotation in the sense that the *sacerdos* or ἱερεύς (*hiereus*) plays religious functions such as interpreting the meaning of events, performing the rituals of the religion and offering sacrifices. The term "priest" in English has assumed the meaning of the Latin *sacerdos* or Greek ἱερεύς (*hiereus*) than πρεσβύτερος (*presbyteros*).

2.2. Historical Development of the Catholic Ministerial Priesthood

The New Testament testifies to the appointment of elders to oversee the affairs of the early Christian community (Acts 14:23; 20:17, 28). The appointed elders were to

---

[31] Eliade, M. (Gen. Ed). *The Encyclopedia of Religion*. Vol. II, New York: Macmillan Publishing Company, 1987. Pg 529

atch over the community and be shepherds over the flock that God purchased with the blood of Jesus and have been entrusted into their care. The functions of the elders included guarding the flock against false teachings that may erupt within the community (Acts 20:30). Some ministers were also appointed by the community to serve the internal needs of the community such as distribution of food (Acts 6:1-6). The apostles and elders laid hands on and prayed over those appointed into various ministries within the early Church (Acts 6:6; 13:1-3, 1 Tim 4:14).

Among all the various ministries within the early Church, we cannot identify a particular priestly ministry in the realistic sense. Ministerial priesthood at that time was "identified with ritual offering of animal and other sacrifices to God, and there was no one in the community designated to do this."[32] Moreover "the first generation of Christians, who were almost all Jews, accepted the legitimacy of the Jewish priesthood, and showed this by continuing to worship at the temple"[33] until its destruction in 70 CE by Roman soldiers and consequently the end of the Jewish cultic priesthood.

According to Martos, a Jewish Christian who lived in Rome composed a response to the troubling questions that were raised after the destruction of the Temple. In his response, the author developed the idea that the crucifixion of Jesus was a perfect sacrifice to God which replaced the temple offerings. The priest and victim of the sacrifice was Jesus himself and his priesthood superseded that of the Jewish religion because he is not a priest by ancestry but a high priest of a new and eternal covenant between God and his people, a high priest of the same order as Melchizedek, whose priesthood had no beginning and no end. [The Church was then seen as the replacement of the old Israel with] A new priesthood and a new high priest, by his perfect life and sacrificial death had become the perfect mediator between God and man (Heb 3:1-10:18).[34]

The priesthood of Jesus Christ is a new and better covenant of which he himself becomes the mediator by virtue of his submission and willing offering of himself by embracing death by the cross. He is the only and unique mediator whose sacrifice reconciles God and humanity. The superiority of the new covenant to the old is based on the eternity of its priesthood that is in Jesus Christ.[35] The author of the letter to the Hebrews emphasizes that Jesus is a royal priest, whose death has been the ultimate

<hr>

[32]J. Martos, *Doors to the Sacred: A Historical Introduction to the Sacraments in the Catholic Church*, New York: Image Books, 1982, 464.

[33]J. Martos, *Doors to the Sacred*, 464.

[34]J. Martos, *Doors to the Sacred*, 464.

[35]Cf. M.M. Bourke, "The Epistle to the Hebrews," in *The New Jerome Biblical Commentary*, London: Burns and Oates, 1995.

sacrifice that had rendered continuation of animal sacrifice ineffective. He presents Christianity as a perfect replacement of the old Israel. Christians therefore thought of themselves as constituting the new people of God which was clearly different and separate from Judaism, and as a result became God's covenanted people who needed to replace the Jewish bloody sacrifice.

The needed replacement, as attested by R. Brown was found "when the Eucharist was seen as unbloody sacrifice replacing the bloody sacrifices no longer offered in the now-destroyed Temple."[36] As early as the end of the first century or the beginning of the second century, Christians identified the Eucharist not just a sacrifice, but "as an unbloody sacrifice replacing the bloody sacrifices."[37] Brown reiterated that *Didache* 14 instructs believers to "assemble on the Lord's Day, breaking bread and celebrating the Eucharist; but first confess your sins that your sacrifice [*thysia*] may be a pure one … for it was of this the Lord spoke 'Everywhere and always offer me a pure sacrifice.'"[38] So far as the second century Christian community thought of the Eucharist in a sacrificial context, it was only appropriate to recognize whoever presided over the celebration as a priest who led the worshipping community in offering sacrifice. This recognition given to the one who presided over the celebration significantly contributed to the emergence of the concept of ministerial priesthood alongside the episcopate and diaconate. These offices: episcopate, presbyterate and diaconate emerged as the most important ministries during the second century.[39]

Consequently, Macquarrie could assert that "in the first few centuries, throughout the whole Church, the various kinds of ministry of which we read in the New Testament had become consolidated into the familiar three orders of bishops, priests and deacons."[40] He further elucidates that "the bishops were thought of as the successors of the apostles, who were supposed to have founded [...] the principal sees of the ancient Church; the priests (or presbyters) corresponds to the pastors indifferently called 'bishops' or 'presbyters' in the New Testament; while the deacons represented those inferior orders of ministry which we can also see in the New Testament."[41] It seems that the idea of the bishops being the successors of the apostles is more of tradition than any clear biblical evidence.

---

[36]R.E. Brown, *Priest and Bishop: Biblical Reflections*, New York: Paulist Press, 1970, 19.

[37]R.E. Brown, *Priests and Bishops*, 17-19.

[38]R.E. Brown, *Priests and Bishops*, 18.

[39] P. McGoldrick, "Sacrament of Orders," in *The New Dictionary of Sacramental Worship*, Minnesota: The Liturgical Press, 1990, 898.

[40]J. Macquarrie, *Principles of Christian Theology*, 2nd ed, New York: Charles Scribner's Sons, 1977, 431.

[41]J. Macquarrie, *Principles of Christian Theology*, 431.

2.2.1. The Bishops

The title "bishop" is translated from the Greek word *episkopos*, which means "overseer", the bishop, therefore is an overseer of God's flock. The bishop ought to be wholesome and exhibit if not all, most of the qualities that Paul enumerated in his letters to Timothy and Titus (1 Tim 3:1-8; Titus 1:6-9). The title "bishop" was used to describe "the function of the presbyter (elder)"[42] in the New Testament (NT). The implication of such an opinion is a lack of clear distinction between the bishop and the presbyter; the latter could be referred to as bishop due to his functions. The bishop is a presbyter who presides over gatherings of presbyters. Functioning in this manner earns him the title bishop. In his contribution to the issue of any distinction between presbyters and bishops, Ratzinger postulates that, Jewish Christian leaders were referred to as presbyters while the leaders of the Gentile churches were referred to as "bishops and deacons"[43] for the first time in Philippians 1:1. This postulation assumes no clear distinction between the two. McKenzie also affirms the position that there is no clear distinction between the bishop and the presbyter as there is between the former and the deacon.[44]

2.2.2. The Deacon

Some theologians including Macquarrie postulate that the diaconate was the least among the three clearly defined special ministries in the NT and recognize its prototype in the ministry of the seven i.e. Stephen and his companions in Acts 6:1-7.[45] Burge also traces the beginning of the diaconate to the appointment of the seven whose primary duty was to help with the distribution of food in order for the apostles to continue effectively with preaching.[46] Although the seven were called to "service" (Acts 6:1, 4), Luke, the author of Acts, does not refer to the seven as deacons however tradition ascribes the institution of the diaconate to the choice of the seven and their praying over by the apostles.[47]

---

[42]P. Toon, "Bishop," in *Evangelical Dictionary of Theology*, 2nd ed. Michigan: Baker Academic, 2001, 170.

[43]J. Ratzinger, *On the Nature of the Priesthood* (Online).

[44]J.L. McKenzie, *Dictionary of the Bible*, London: Cassell Publishers Limited, 1968, 97.

[45]J. Macquarrie, *Principles of Christian Theology*, 432-433.

[46]G.M. Burge, "Deacon, Deaconess," in *Evangelical Dictionary of Theology*, 2nd ed., Michigan: Baker Academic, 2001, 320.

[47]J.P. Dunn, *Priesthood: A Re-Examination of the Roman Catholic Theology of the Presbyterate*, New York: Alba House, 1990, 50.

2.2.3. The Priests

Wallace and other authors associate the presbyterate with the beginning of the Church, "taking their [presbyters] place along with the apostles, prophets, and teachers." [48] He identifies the presbyterate at Jerusalem with James in "the government of the local Church after the manner of the synagogue" (Acts 11:3; 21:18). Gleeson affirms the position that the presbyterate was "a form of leadership in Jewish synagogues (Acts 15:22) and practiced by the first Christians, who were themselves Jews."[49] The presbyters functioned as overseers in the absence of apostles and essentially as teachers and preachers (1 Tim 5:17). We can deduce that the kind of presbyterate practiced by the first Christians is not same in essence as today's ministerial priests.

In addition to the happenings in the second century, Gelpi also observes the emergence of *monepiskopos*, which was a reference to one bishop presiding over a local Christian community; later on, "episcopal supervision of Christian cult evolved into episcopal control."[50] By the third century bishops were often (and rarely presbyters) referred to as high priests of the new covenant. He opines that the tendency of referring to the bishops and presbyters as priests attained its highest point during the fourth century through a theological movement called Sacerdotalism. For him, Sacerdotalist theology was a reflection of the new political status of Christianity as a religion recognized by the Roman Empire and later as the sole lawful religion of the state.

The theologians within the movement (Sacerdotalism) intended to guard episcopal authority from imperial invasion. Basil of Caesarea is cited to be the first theologian to lay the foundation of the theology of Christian ministerial priesthood by teaching that "bishops participate directly in the priestly authority of Christ in church matters in a manner analogous to the emperor's direct participation in divine authority in secular matters."[51] Sacerdotalist theologians also portrayed bishops as the Levitical priests of the new covenant. This kind of teachings gave bishops priestly functions different in essence from that of the priesthood of the baptized or the entire faith community. Within the fourth century, presbyters or priests became second in terms

---

[48] R.S. Wallace, "Elder," in *Evangelical Dictionary of Theology*, 2nd ed., Michigan: Baker Academic, 2001, 369.

[49] B. Gleeson, "Ordained Persons and their Ministries: New Testament Foundations and Variations," *Australian eJournal of Theology*, 7, 2006, 8.

[50] D.L. Gelpi, "Priesthood," in *The New Dictionary of Sacramental Worship (editor: Peter E. Fink)*, Minnesota: The Liturgical Press, 1990, 1015.

[51] D.L. Gelpi, "Priesthood," 1015.

of clerical authority to the bishops as the former began to preside over the Eucharistic celebration mostly in the rural areas where bishops could not be present[52].

Other authors assert that the scholastic theologians of the Late Middle Ages identified priests as the foremost ministers of the Christian Eucharistic sacrifice. For the theologians, the priests were endowed with power by ordination to transubstantiate bread and wine, forgive sin, baptize, and administer the last unction or the sacrament of anointing of the sick.[53]

Priests in medieval Christianity "were the primary mediators between God and man in almost every aspect of Christian life."[54] Thus priesthood in that period was mostly thought as "sacramental, liturgical and cultic ministry in terms of authority, office, and jurisdiction."[55] Some theologians of that period limited the priestly function to the offering of the Mass and considered other functions such as preaching and administration as mere ministerial functions that are not necessarily priestly, and this kind of thoughts indirectly might have prepared the ground for the Protestant rejection of the ministerial priesthood.

The Second Vatican Council affirms that by the sacred power of Orders, priests are empowered to offer sacrifice and forgive sins and the ordained are to attend to their priestly duties in the name of Christ. The Council taught that the office of the priestly "ministry has been handed down, in a lesser degree indeed to the priests" (PO, 2) through the bishops who are successors of the apostles. The bishops as successors participate in the mission that Jesus handed over to the apostles. Jesus sends out the bishops just as he sent out the apostles. The priests are therefore working together with the bishops to accomplish the mission. They share in the priesthood of the bishops. The Council made it clearer that priests "can be co-workers of the episcopal order for the proper fulfilment of the apostolic mission entrusted to priests by Christ" (PO, 2).

From the discussion so far, we observe that the ministerial priesthood has been going through gradual developments since the second century. From the fourth century through the Middle Ages to the Second Vatican Council, the priest has always been considered as the one endowed with power to preside over the Eucharist and administer the sacraments. The Second Vatican Council also places emphasis on the preaching of the Gospel as a priestly duty and not a mere ministerial function. The focus of our discussion would now be shifted to the theology of priesthood

---

[52] D.L. Gelpi, "Priesthood," 1015.

[53] Cf. D.L. Gelpi, "Priesthood," 1015.

[54] J. Martos, *Doors to the Sacred*, 499.

[55] J. Martos, *Doors to the Sacred*, 499.

2.3. Theology of the Catholic Priesthood

The notion of priesthood is inseparably tied to that of worship. The notion of worship of a deity and priesthood are ancient phenomena that are as old as humankind. It is therefore not out of place for a community to appoint one of its members as a priest to organize and lead in the worship of a deity. The danger here is that there could be a notion of priesthood which could be of human standard without any divine essence. "The Gospel does not establish a religion which mankind set up for the worship of God, but a religion which God himself came down to reveal."[56] The priest in this religion is not an ordinary man chosen by the community to lead and organize worship, but Jesus Christ who is the sole mediator between God and man. The priesthood of Jesus Christ is not a mere human invention; it is divinely revealed. The Catholic ministerial priesthood is therefore derived from this divine revelation and the priest with his functions can only be comprehended through the priesthood of Jesus Christ.

It is clearly stated in the Second Vatican Council's document that the Lord Jesus Christ "has established ministers among his faithful to unite them together in one body in which 'not all the members have the same function' (Rom 12:4). These ministers in the society of the faithful are able by the sacred power of Orders to […] perform their priestly office publicly for men in the name of Christ" (PO, 2). The Council affirms and elucidates that Christ instituted the sacramental priesthood and differentiates it from the common or universal priesthood that is attained by baptism. The difference is known by virtue of the former functioning publicly as priest in the name of Christ.

In support of the position that the ministerial priesthood was instituted by Christ, Kloppenburg explains that the Council of Trent affirmed: "Christ at the Last Supper, wishing to leave his Church a visible sacrifice, gave his body and blood to the Apostles, 'making them priests of the New Testament at that time'"[57]. Christ made the Apostles priests while instituting the Eucharist or the Last Supper in order for them to fulfil the command he gave for the continuation of the Supper in his memorial (Lk 22:19). The Apostles also transmitted the power to preside over the Eucharist to their disciples and the same power is transmitted to Catholic priests at Ordination. Hahn therefore could affirm:

> In time, those men [the apostles] passed on their priestly ministry through a sacramental rite: the laying of hands (see Acts 6:6). The apostles ritually placed their hands upon the men who would be their co-

---

[56] J.M. Perrin, *The Minister of Christ*, Dublin: M.H. Gill & Son Ltd, 1964, 19.

[57] B. Kloppenburg, *The Ecclesiology of Vatican II*, Chicago: Franciscan Herald Press, 1974, 273.

workers and successors. By this rite of ordination, the apostles conferred the gift of priesthood on a new generation (see 2 Tim 1:6). And so it has passed through the millennia, to the priests who serve us today. Through this action, those who are ordained receive the Spirit of Jesus Christ, and so they receive power to perform actions that are properly divine.[58]

The imposition of hands is a symbol of invocation of the Holy Spirit upon those men who became co-workers and successors of the apostles. It also signified the new office or order that those men were to assume. Granting that the same power given to the Apostles had been transmitted to them, then all ministerial priests are partakers in the office of the Apostles implying that they are obligated to continue the celebration of the Eucharist and also continue the mission of the twelve as mandated by Jesus Christ. In this mission the priests are called to the proclamation of the Gospel to the entire human race. The focus of the proclamation of the Gospel is the conversion of unbelievers to faith in Jesus Christ the high priest.

Jesus Christ the high priest established the ministerial priesthood and those belonging to this priesthood attend to their priestly duties publicly in the name of the one who established the sacred office. Kloppenburg affirms:

> The mystery of Christ is present and operative only through the ministerial priesthood. The priest, the man chosen by God, is the visible sign, the means and living instrument, of Christ the eternal Priest amid the community of believers. Through the special sacrament he receives, the priest is ontologically qualified to build, sanctify, and rule the Church in the name and person of Christ and with his authority. As a possessor of genuine sacred power that is to be exercised publicly for men in the name of Christ, the priest can present himself to the people as the authentic representative or Vicar of Christ, in whose name and with whose authority he preaches, sanctifies and directs.[59]

The priest who presides over the Eucharist does not play the role of Jesus, rather he allows himself to be taken over and be used by Jesus Christ who is the source of all priesthood and the true celebrant. However, other men can only have a share in that priesthood insofar as Christ the High Priest empowers them. Whenever the priest proclaims the Word, forgives sins, and transubstantiates bread and wine, he is only acting *in persona Christi* and *persona ecclesiae* — "in the person of Christ and in the

---

[58]S. Hahn, *Many are Called: Rediscovering the Glory of the Priesthood,* New York: Doubleday, 2010, 33.
[59]B. Kloppenburg, *The Ecclesiology of Vatican II,* 292.

person of the Church." During these rites the power of Christ and the power of the worshipping community are concentrated on him.[60]

The implication is that the priest derives his authority from Christ and the Church. In this context, the Church is a worshipping community of which the priest is a member. Being a priest and a member of "the body of Christ" does not make him the head because Christ is the sole head of the body. What makes the ordained priest different from the lay priests or other members of "the body of Christ" is his triple function of Sanctification, Teaching and Governing. He is a Sanctifier because he offers sacrifice, as a Teacher he proclaims the Gospel and as a King he governs and guards the properties of the Church.

Hahn affirms that, "through holy orders, the Church's priests are conformed to Christ in a unique way. In our priestly family, they serve in the person and place of the divine first born, the only begotten son of God. It is from him, above all others that they learn to be priests. They succeed as they imitate him."[61] We can deduce that the ministerial priest is not a man of his own; rather a man of Christ and a man for all those who also share in the priesthood of Christ through baptism. The priest is "conformed to Christ in a unique way [to] serve in the person and place" of Christ.

One significant role of the priest, as stipulated by McCauley, is to be the Christian community's "public reminder of the word and action of Christ."[62] In his capacity as "a simple reminder" the priest is obliged to relive Christ's priesthood in all spheres of life. The Christian community must be reminded of who Christ is through the actions of the priest. In living and proclamation of the Gospel, the celebration of the Eucharist and administration of other Sacraments, the priest responds to his vocation and becomes the "simple reminder" of who Christ is to the Christian community.

We can with Burghardt outline four general functions of the priest which are that "the priest is ordained to proclaim the word of God"; he is to build the Christian community by assuming his leadership responsibility. Furthermore as an ordained priest, he must render service to humanity and most importantly the priest is ordained to preside over the Eucharist, which is the fulcrum of the Catholic faith.[63]

In his contribution to Catholic theology of the priesthood, Power emphasizes that the priest is also assigned through "ordination to the threefold ministry of Word,

---

[60]W.J. O'Malley, *Sacraments: Rites of Passage*, Chicago: Thomas Moore, 1995, 223.

[61]S. Hahn, *Many are Called*, 134.

[62]G. McCauley, "The Priest: A Simple Reminder," in *The Sacraments: Readings in Contemporary Sacramental Theology*, New York: Alba House, 1981, 177.

[63]W.J. Burrghardt, "What is a Priest?" in *The Sacraments: Readings in Contemporary Sacramental Theology*, New York: Alba House, 1981, 168.

sacrament and pastoral care."[64] The inference is that priests are ordained to proclaim the Gospel and this should not be sacrificed for anything. Furthermore, they are also ordained to administer the sacraments and shepherd the people of God entrusted to their care. In addition, priests ought to offer guidance and counselling to the people of God, as they are obliged by their ministry to do so.

Discussing the origin of the ministerial priesthood, Ekem, a protestant theologian affirms that the Catholic Church considers her priesthood as a direct derivation from the Christological priesthood expounded in the letter to the Hebrews. The priests of the Catholic Church are in a realistic sense "participants in Christ's unique priestly sacrifice, serving as mediators through whom the latter is vividly brought home to others [...] during celebration of Mass."[65] It is very significant to note that priests being "participants in Christ's unique priestly sacrifice" does not imply that they played a role in Christ's sacrifice of willingly giving up himself to be crucified for the salvation of all humanity. Rather it should be seen in the light of re-enacting the exact sacrifice of the crucifixion at Calvary whenever they preside over the celebration of the Holy Eucharist or the Mass. In other words being "participants in Christ's unique sacrifice" means that through the grace that they receive in the sacrament of ordination, they act *in persona Christi*.

In contrast to the understanding of the ministerial priesthood, Mathew posits that the doctrine of the priesthood of all believers nullifies the existence of what he refers to as "unbiblical doctrine of sacerdotalism and the existence of a Brahman-like priestly class within the church."[66] However, Hardon postulates that the priesthood of Christ is the sole fundamental priesthood in the Church and all other priests are participants in that Christological priesthood. The participation is of two forms namely, the royal priesthood of all the baptized and the ministerial priesthood which is realized in the sacrament of Holy Orders. Hardon defends the ministerial priesthood by referring to the Last Supper, arguing, in that very night the Lord instituted not only the Last Supper but also the priesthood. His argument underscores the notion that the Last Supper and the priesthood are inseparable and places the Last Supper in a sacrificial context. In such a sacrificial context, it will take only priests to preside over the celebration of the Last Supper.

---

[64] D.N. Power, "Order," in *Systematic Theology: Roman Catholic Perspectives*, Vol. II, Minneapolis: Fortress Press, 1991, 292.

[65] J.D.K. Ekem, *Priesthood in Context: a study of Priesthood in some Christian and Primal Communities of Ghana and its Relevance for Mother-Tongue Biblical Interpretation*, Accra: SonLife Press, 2009, 118.

[66] P.G. Mathew, *The Priesthood of All Believers* [on line] (1996) available at: http://members.dcn.org [accessed in March 2011].

P.G. Matthew's position against the ministerial priesthood as seen in the above paragraph suggests that any baptized Christian can preside over the celebration of the Last Supper that the Lord instituted. This may create chaos and indiscipline in the Church as each member may claim the right to officiate the celebration by virtue of his baptism. Again, on this position, we observe that in the celebration of the Last Supper in protestant traditions such as the Methodist and the Presbyterian churches, it is always officiated by an ordained minister and not just any baptized member of the community even though their understanding of the Last Supper is different from that of the Catholic tradition. Those who become priests in the Catholic tradition are those that the Lord graciously grants the gift of priestly vocation.

2.4. The Vocation to the Catholic Priesthood

Vocation means a "calling". Vocation is a personal call offered freely and must be accepted willingly. Though the Christian vocation is a gift from God to humanity, the family contributes to the individual's realization of his vocation to the priesthood by bringing him up in the faith. In support of this opinion, Bushman in his commentary on the Second Vatican Council's decree on formation of priests, *Optatam Totius* points out that "a vocation to the priesthood has as its foundation a vibrant faith which ideally develops in the family"[67]. The vocation to the Catholic priesthood is a gift from God that "is never bestowed outside or independently of the Church". John Paul II exhorts that the priestly vocation "is a call, by the Sacrament of Holy Orders received in the Church, to place oneself at the service of the People of God with a particular belonging and configuration to Jesus Christ and with the authority of acting 'in the name and in the person' of him who is the Head and Shepherd of the Church"[68]. He teaches that each priest receives his personal call from the Lord Jesus Christ through the Church as a gracious gift. The priestly vocation is characterized primarily by a divine initiated dialogue through which the individual responds. God is the one who first takes the initiative to call the individual. This is evident in how he called the prophets of old (Jer 1:4-5) and how Jesus called the disciples who later became the apostles (Mk 3: 13). The call to the Catholic priesthood is a continuous process that does not end even after ordination. The Lord continues to call even those who have received ordination to accept their vocations as priests daily and work towards that sacred vocation they have willingly embraced.

---

[67] Trouve M.L., (Gen. Ed.) *The Sixteen Documents of Vatican II (Introductions by Douglas G. Bushman).* Boston: Pauline Books & Media. 1999. Pg 328.
[68] John Paul II, *Pastores Dabo Vobis: Post-Synodal Apostolic Exhortation on the Formation of Priests in the circumstances of the present day.* London: Catholic Truth Society. 1992. (*PDV 35*)

2.5.0. The Formation of Candidates for the Catholic Priesthood

Jesus called twelve men among his disciples to be with him whom he also made apostles (Mk 3:13-15). These men were with him throughout his ministry during which he taught and formed them into the very people he wanted them to be. Jesus taught them how to pray (Lk 11:1-4) and gave them insight to some of the parables he used in his teachings which the crowd were not privileged to comprehend (Mt 13:10-23). He gave this special formation to the twelve because he knew he would later send them out for the proclamation of the kingdom. The twelve that he chose spent enough time with him and had intimacy with him. The Catholic Church believes that Jesus continues to call people to be sent out for the same mission. The Catholic Church therefore learns from the example of Jesus by giving adequate and proper formation to those he (Jesus) calls in our age at the various Seminaries.

John Paul II explains: "the 'seminary' in its different forms, and analogously the 'house' of formation for religious priests, more than a place, a material space, should be a spiritual place, a way of life, an atmosphere that fosters and ensures a process of formation, so that the person who is called to the priesthood by God may become, with the Sacrament of Orders, a living image of Jesus Christ, Head and Shepherd of the Church"[69]. During the formation period, candidates for the priesthood are consciously trained to offer their entire being to Jesus, learn from him and follow him as the apostles did, and also develop intimate relationship with him through daily prayer and meditation on the Scriptures and Eucharistic celebration.

He continued to elaborate on the Christological perspective of the formation to the priesthood when he acknowledged the originality and specificity of the significance

> [. ..] of the formation of candidates for the priesthood, [...] 'To live in the seminary, which is a school of the Gospel, means to follow Christ as the Apostles did. You are led by Christ into the service of God the Father and of all people, under the guidance of the Holy Spirit. Thus, you become more like Christ the Good Shepherd in order better to serve the Church and the world as a priest. In preparing for priesthood, we learn how to respond from the heart to Christ's basic question: 'Do you love me?' (Jn21:15). For the future priest the answer can only mean total self-giving'.[70]

Catholic priests are given holistic formation to aid give themselves up totally to Christ and humanity. In apostolic exhortation, John Paul II emphasizes on four major

---

[69] (PDV 42)

[70] (PDV 42)

pillars of the holistic formation offered in all the seminaries and these are – human, spiritual, intellectual and pastoral formations[71].

2.5.1. Human Formation

The human formation of the candidate is the foundation of the priestly formation without which the future ministry of the candidate would be in chaos. Proper human formation leads the candidate onto auto discovery (i.e. self-knowledge), development of good relationships and affective maturity. John Paul II elucidates that "the priest, who is called to be a 'living image' of Jesus Christ, Head and Shepherd of the Church, should seek to reflect in himself, as far as possible, the human perfection which shines forth in the Incarnate Son of God and which is reflected with particular liveliness in his attitudes towards others as […] narrated in the Gospels"[72].

The priest cannot pursue his ministry without having any relationship with humankind as he proclaims the Gospel and administers the Sacraments "in the name and the person of Christ" to the faith community. The priest is ordained to perform his priestly duties among humankind and acts on behalf of the latter in relation to God (Heb 5:1) and this cannot be achieved if the priest does not relate well to those he had been ordained for. In performing his duties, the priest must avail himself as a bridge and not an obstacle to those who are drawing closer to the Lord.

For this reason and others, the candidate for the priesthood is formed in a way that enables him develop his human personality in order to "know the depths of the human heart, to perceive difficulties and problems, to make meeting and dialogue easy, to create trust and cooperation, to express serene and objective judgments"[73]. In addition, the candidate is formed to cultivate good human qualities such as loyalty, respect for humanity (for the old, young, rich and poor) honesty, compassion, affability, generosity, forgiveness, justice and prudence to enable him bear problems that may be associated with pastoral responsibilities in the priestly ministry. The priest is called therefore to be a father to the people and as a father; it is of great importance to relate well to his "children". The candidates is also formed in areas of moral conscience to enable him appreciate the need to be obedient to moral obligations and guide the consciences of those who would be entrusted into his care. All these human qualities are intrinsically bound up to what we call "affective maturity".

---

[71] (PDV 42)

[72] (PDV 43)
[73] (PDV 43)

ffective maturity "is a significant and decisive factor in the formation of candidates for the priesthood"[74]. Affective maturity is achieved through "education in true and responsible love" and it assumes an awareness of the central place of love in the life of humankind. In the encyclical *Redemptor Hominis*, he asserts, "Man cannot live without love. He remains a being that is incomprehensible for himself, his life is senseless, if love is not revealed to him, if he does not encounter love, if he does not experience it and make it his own, if he does not participate intimately in it"[75]. John Paul II explains that this kind of love must be holistic in the sense that it should entail the whole being including the physical, psychic and spiritual aspects "which is expressed in the 'nuptial meaning' of the human body [...] to which a person gives himself to another and takes the other to himself" [76]. When this is well understood and well grasped, the truth about human love would be realized and appreciated. In a society where love and sex have been reduced merely to bodily selfish pleasure, candidates for the priesthood are offered education on human sexuality that presents and recognizes chastity as a "virtue that develops a person's authentic maturity and makes him [...] capable of respecting and fostering the nuptial meaning of the body"[77]. Again, in his apostolic exhortation, John Paul II affirms:

> Education for responsible love and the affective maturity of the person are totally necessary for those who, like the priest are called to celibacy that is, to offer with the grace of the Spirit and the free response of one's own will the whole of one's love and care to Jesus Christ and to his Church. In view of the commitment to celibacy, affective maturity should bring to human relationships of serene friendship and deep brotherliness a strong, lively and personal love for Jesus Christ. As the Synod Fathers have written, 'a love for Christ, which overflows into a dedication to everyone, is of the greatest importance in developing affective maturity. Thus the candidate, who is called to celibacy, will find in affective maturity a firm support to live in chastity in faithfulness and joy'[78].

It is therefore imperatively important that during the priesthood formation, candidates grow and develop healthy relationships, through accepting or receiving and out love

---

[74] (PDV 44)

[75] John Paul II, *Redemptor Hominis*. Huntington: Our Sunday Visitor Publishing Division. 1996. *RH* 10.1).

[76] (PDV 44)

[77] (PDV 44)

[78] (PDV 44)

responsibility. This is the basis for developing a genuine interpersonal relationship with all categories of people and sexes without discrimination or compromise.

2.5.2. Spiritual Formation

Since only genuine love generates life, then the human formation based on such a fundamental element which is love must lead to an in-depth relationship with the source of love which is God. Consequently we can affirm with John Paul II that through revelation and Christian experience, spiritual formation of a candidate to the priesthood "possesses the unmistakable originality which derives from evangelical newness"[79]. He again emphasizes that spiritual formation "is the work of the Holy Spirit and engages a person in his totality. It introduces him to a deep communion with Jesus Christ, the Good Shepherd, and leads to the total submission of one's life to the Spirit, in a filial attitude towards the Father and a trustful attachment to the Church"[80]. Spiritual formation helps to appreciate the work of Jesus on the cross and draws the candidate into a deeper communion with him. The spiritual formation of the future priest "unifies and gives life to his *being* a priest and his *acting* as a priest"[81].

The essential content needed for the spiritual formation of the candidates for the priesthood is highlighted in the Second Vatican Council's document *Optatam Totius*:

> The spiritual training [formation] should be imparted in such a way that the students might learn to live in an intimate and unceasing union with the Father through His Son Jesus Christ in the Holy Spirit. Conformed to Christ the Priest through their sacred ordination, they should be accustomed to adhere to Him as friends, in an intimate companionship, their whole life through. They should so live His Paschal Mystery themselves that they can initiate into it the flock committed to them. They should be taught to seek Christ in the faithful meditation on God's Word, in the active participation in the sacred mysteries of the Church, especially in the Eucharist and in the divine office, in the bishop who sends them and in the people to whom they are sent, especially the poor, the children, the sick, the sinners and the unbelievers. They should love and venerate with a filial trust the most Blessed Virgin Mary, who was

---

[79] (PDV 45)
[80] (PDV 45)
[81] (PDV 45)

given as mother to the disciple by Christ Jesus as He was dying on the cross[82].

From the text, we realize that the Council demands that candidates for the priesthood should be developed "to live in an intimate union with the Father through His Son Jesus Christ in the Holy Spirit". It implies that the Council places a demand on candidates to develop a personal relationship with the Holy Trinity. Out of this relationship, they could perceive a proper conception of the triune God through their personal experience. This kind of intimacy that the Council seeks to promote begins at Baptism and continues to be nourished through the Sacraments, especially, daily reception of the Eucharist. When the priest is able to develop and maintain such intimacy with the Holy Trinity, he would then offer good spiritual guidance to the faithful and encourage them to pursue and deepen their personal relationship with the Lord as that kind of relationship had already been initiated at their baptism.

The Council, in the text again spells out the Christological dimension of the formation to the priesthood by insisting that candidates for the priesthood "should be taught to seek Christ". The Council provides the path that should be taken in seeking Christ. The path involves "faithful meditation on God's Word, in the active participation in the sacred mysteries of the Church, especially in the Eucharist and in the divine office, [...] and in the people to whom they are sent, especially the poor, the children, the sick, the sinners and the unbelievers"[83].

In meditating upon the Word, the future priest hears in his inner most part the voice of the Master he seeks to follow and also by participating in the sacred mysteries of the church, he experiences the mysteries of God. Seeking Christ in the poor and the marginalized also helps the future priest not to discriminate in his ministry because in doing so he might not recognize the Christ that he seeks. The candidates for the priesthood are to seek Christ daily and when they find him, others are to be invited to encounter that same Christ. Being a priest in a church that has the sole mission of evangelization one cannot refuse to seek Christ daily, as he ought to witness Christ to those who do not know Him and even those who lack a deeper knowledge of who the Christ is.

---

[82] *Optatam Totius (OT* 8)
[83] *Optatam Totius (OT* 8)

2.5.3. Intellectual Formation

In responding to the call to evangelization, priests are to proclaim the Gospel of Christ to all and sundry. In a sophisticated world with highly sophisticated minds, priests have a sacred duty to champion the course of bringing the light of the Gospel to such minds. This duty makes it a necessity for candidates for the Catholic priesthood to seek a high level of intellectual formation. Intellectual formation "is a fundamental demand of man's intelligence by which he 'participates in the light of God's mind' and seeks to acquire a wisdom which in turn opens to and is directed towards knowing and adhering to God"[84]. The future priest shares his benefits from intellectual formation together with the community that would be placed under his care. When with the human formation the future priest integrates the product of intellectual formation with a Christian spirituality that entails a personal encounter with Jesus, he becomes very effective in the pastoral duties that would be assigned to him.

One of the most vital and greatest stages of the intellectual formation is the introduction of candidates to the study of Philosophy, which enables candidates to appreciate "the links between the great philosophical questions and mysteries of salvation which are studied in theology under the guidance of higher light of faith"[85]. John Paul II posits:

> Only a sound philosophy can help candidates for the priesthood to develop a reflective awareness of the fundamental relationship that exists between the human spirit and truth, that truth which is revealed to us fully in Jesus Christ. Nor must one underestimate the importance of philosophy as a guarantee of that 'certainty of truth' which is the only firm basis for a total giving of oneself to Jesus and to the Church. [...] Philosophy greatly helps the candidate to enrich his intellectual formation in the 'cult of truth', namely, in a kind of loving veneration of the truth, which leads one to recognize that the truth is not created or measured by man but is given to man as a gift by the Supreme Truth, God; that, albeit in a limited way and often with difficulty, human reason can reach objective and universal truth, even that relating to God and the radical meaning of existence; and that faith itself cannot do without reason and the effort of 'thinking through' its content as that great mind

---

[84] (PDV 51)

[85] (PDV 52)

Augustine bore witness: 'I wished to see with my mind what I have believed, and I have argued and labored greatly'[86].

In the study of Philosophy, the candidate realizes the identity of the priest and "his apostolic and missionary commitments are closely linked to the question about the nature of truth"[87]. Most importantly, the study of Philosophy prepares the candidate for the study of sacred doctrine of theology, which is the centre of priestly intellectual formation. The study of theology deepens the faith of the candidate by intriguing in him the desire to question and critically reflect on his own faith. It deepens the faith by leading to a deeper personal relationship with Jesus Christ in the Church and this would enhance the pastoral ministry of the future priest. In addition, candidates are introduced to the study of human sciences such as Sociology, Anthropology and Psychology.

2.5.4. Pastoral Formation

The purpose of the entire formation given to candidates for the priesthood is to usher them into "communion with the charity of Jesus Christ the good shepherd"[88], hence there cannot be a holistic formation without pastoral formation although various aspects of the formation has pastoral character. The Second Vatican Council declares that "the entire training of the students [candidates for the priesthood] should be oriented to the formation of true shepherds of souls after the model of our Lord Jesus Christ, teacher, priest and shepherd [...] Therefore, all the forms of training, spiritual, intellectual, disciplinary, are to be ordered with concerted effort towards this pastoral end,"[89]. Pastoral formation like the other pillars of the formation "develops by means of mature reflection and practical application". For John Paul II it needs to be learnt through pastoral or practical theology and that is

> a scientific reflection on the Church as she is built up daily, by the power of the Spirit, in history; on the Church as the 'universal sacrament of salvation' as a living sign and instrument of the salvation wrought by Christ through the word, the sacraments and the service of charity. Pastoral theology is not just an art [...] it is theological in its own right

---

86 (PDV 52)
87 (PDV 52)
88 (PDV 57)
89 (*OT* 4)

because it receives from faith the principles and criteria for the pastoral action of the Church in history, [...][90].

The study of pastoral theology is to illumine the practical aspect of the pastoral formation through "involvement in certain pastoral services which the candidates to the priesthood should carry out with a necessary progression and always in harmony with their educational commitments. It is a question of pastoral 'experiences', which can come together in a real programme of 'pastoral training' which can last a considerable amount of time"[91]. The sense of awareness that pastoral formation is not a matter of "mere apprenticeship" focused on introducing a candidate to some field techniques for the *job* is imbided in him by initiating the candidate into "the sensitivity of being a shepherd, in the conscious and mature assumption of his responsibilities, in the interior habit of evaluating problems and establishing priorities and looking for solutions on the basis of honest motivations of faith and according to the theological demands inherent in pastoral work"[92].

A complete pastoral formation would lead the candidate for the priesthood to the knowledge that the existence of the Church is by the work of the divine and it is only the divine who sustains the Church. This would prompt the future priest not to rely on his own abilities in sustaining the Church but the Spirit of God. The pastoral formation again introduces the candidate to the communion and missionary dimension of the Church. In this case, the future priest would know how to relate to all members of the Church – bishops, priests (secular), deacons, religious priests, brothers and sisters and the laity. The candidate for the priesthood would also be prepared to live the missionary dimension of the church and be ready at all time to evangelize, as the church exists to evangelize.

The four major pillars of the formation of the candidates for the Catholic priesthood are human, spiritual, intellectual and pastoral. A holistic formation of the candidate for Catholic priesthood cannot be completed without these four pillars. After a candidate has been taken through all these pillars of formation successfully and is found worthy of becoming a Catholic priest, he is then presented to the bishop who then administers to him the sacrament of sacred Orders. Haligan observes that the bishop ordains the candidate into the diaconate Order[93]. The candidate becomes a transitional deacon for a minimum period of six months; afterwards the deacon then receives the Sacrament of Ordination to the priesthood.

---

[90] (PDV 52)

[91] (PDV 57)

[92] (PDV 58)

[93] Halligan, N. 1986. Pg 143

.6. The Rites of Ordination to the Catholic Priesthood

Ordination is "the act of consecrating men to be the sacred ministers for the worship of God and for the sanctification of all people"[94]. Schmaus posits that ordination to the Catholic priesthood differentiates the priest from the people within the Christian community. He refers to the priest's ordination as "the sacrament of differentiation within the people of God"[95]. Halligan identifying with such thoughts also affirms, "By their vocation and ordination priests of the New Testament are truly set apart in a certain sense within the midst of God's people […] that they may be totally dedicated to the work for which the Lord has raised them up"[96]. The sacramental character of ordination does not only distinguish the ordained from the non-ordained but also configures the ordained to the person of Christ and enables him to act in *persona Christi* (person of Christ). Halligan supports the assertion that when men are ordained to the priesthood "they are signed with a specific character and are configured to Christ the Priest and are thus able to act in the person of Christ our Head"[97]. It is important to note that once the sacrament of ordination is validly conferred, it cannot be repeated and it is irreversible because of the "specific character" it imprints on the individual.

The power to ordain is resided in a consecrated bishop. Ordination to the priesthood can only be valid and licit when it is presided over by a consecrated bishop who is in communion with the Church. According to Halligan, the sacrament of ordination ought to be celebrated in a Cathedral church on a Sunday or a holy day of obligation, but due to pastoral reasons it could be celebrated in an ordinary church or even oratory on other days including ordinary weekdays[98]. The celebration of the sacrament of ordination takes place within Holy Mass after the liturgy of the Word and the structure of the rite entails: election, promise of obedience, litany of the saints, imposition of hands and prayer of ordination, investiture with stole and chasuble, anointing of hands, presentation of bread and wine to the newly ordained and kiss of peace.

At the end of the liturgy of the Word begins the election of candidate(s). The candidate for ordination is called to come forward, and a representative of his family presents him to the Church for ordination. The bishop inquires from the candidate of

---

[94] *Catholic Encyclopedia and Dictionary (CD)*. Huntington: Our Sunday Visitor Publishing Division, 1991.

[95] Schmaus, M. Dogma 5: *The Church as Sacrament*. London: Sheed and Ward Inc, 1975, Pg 185

[96] Halligan, N. 1986. Pg 134

[97] Halligan, N. 1986. Pg 143

[98] Halligan, N. 1986. Pg 135

his request and he answers that he seeks for ordination into the priesthood. The bishop inquires of the worthiness of the candidate for the sacrament from a priest who has been involved in the seminary formation. The priest answers in the affirmative and requests that the bishop ordain the candidate. The congregation also gives their consent mostly through clapping and shouts of "Amen". The candidate to be ordained goes before the bishop and makes a promise of obedience. As he does so he kneels before the bishop and places his hands between those of the bishop. The candidate promises to be obedient to the bishop and all his successors. This is followed by the invocation of the Litany of the Saints.

The candidate then prostrates with head towards the altar while the bishop, priests and the whole church kneel and invoke the Litany of the Saints through singing or recitation. This prayer asks for the intercession of the saints in order that God may look favourably upon the candidate for ordination. A prayer follows asking that the Holy Spirit may be poured upon him. While these prayers are being said, the faithful are to join their prayers for the candidate to those of the bishop. The gift of the Holy Spirit is conferred upon the candidate(s) by imposition of hands and through the prayer of ordination.

At the ordination of a priest, the bishop presiding over the celebration imposes his hands on the candidate. All priests present at celebration also impose hands on the candidate in silence as well. The Bishop alone then imposes his hands and says the prayer of consecration or ordination over the candidate. Detscher suggests that the imposition of hands [99] symbolizes that the candidate is to be ordained into the presbyterial college of the local Church and that gives him a "share in the council of the presbyterate"[100]. After the prayer of consecration, the candidate is a priest and is invested properly with the stole and chasuble that are appropriate for the celebration of the Eucharist.

The bishop proceeds to anoint the palms of the new priest. It is a symbol of the anointing of the Holy Spirit that took place through the imposition of hands and the prayer of ordination. It also symbolizes the priest's distinctive participation in Christ's priesthood by the sacrifice he would offer with his hands. Schmaus opines

---

[99]Detscher (1990:909) elucidates that the act of imposition of hands is in keeping with an ancient text found in the *Apostolic Tradition,* which is believed to have been written by Hippolytus. It was declared in *Sacramentum Ordinis* (1947) by Paul XII "the imposition of hands was the sacramental matter of ordination and the epicletic section of each prayer of consecration was the sacramental form of ordination"

[100] Detscher, A.F., "Symbol of Orders". in: *The New Dictionary of Sacramental Worship.* Minnesota: The Liturgical Press, Pg 909.

that the anointing of hands of the new priest was gradually introduced from the eighth century and was generally adopted as element of the ordination rite but until the twelfth century, it was thought of as a separate form of consecration[101].

The new priest is presented with bread on a paten and a chalice of wine. These are the symbols of the priest's duty to offer the sacrifice of the Holy Eucharist and to follow the example of Christ crucified. They are brought up by the lay faithful and presented to a deacon who takes them to the bishop. The bishop then presents them to the newly ordained priest saying, "Accept from the Holy People of God the gifts to be offered to him. Know what you are doing, and imitate the mystery you celebrate, and model your life to the mystery of the Lord's cross"[102]. This gesture emphasizes the close relationship between the rites of ordination and the celebration of the Eucharist. The priest is ordained for the faithful and to offer sacrifice. The primary duty of the priest is to preside over the celebration of the Eucharist.

The bishop and all priests present offer a kiss of peace, which may include hugs and whispering of congratulatory messages to the newly ordained priest(s). This is to acknowledge the admittance of the newly ordained to the rank of a co-worker with the bishop and the other members of the local clergy who assist the bishop in the diocese. The priests welcome the newly ordained as a fellow co-worker in their shared ministry. The normal celebration of the Mass continues with the newly ordained participating fully as co-celebrant. In the Ghanaian certain, the newly ordained priest says a prayer of blessings over the ordaining bishop, formators at the seminary and his parents in the course of the Mass[103]. The newly ordained now enters and participates fully in the life and ministry of the Catholic priesthood.

2.7. The Life and Ministry of Catholic Priests

The Catholic priest may live his own life but not for himself, nor in contradiction with the teachings of the Catholic Church. His life should be in consonance with the dictates of the Gospel. As a priest, he is a representative of the Church and does not act in his own person but in the person of Christ. The Church calls her priests to a life of perfection, invites priests to embrace voluntary poverty, celibacy and obedience to God, through the church, whose direct representative in this context are the pope, bishops, superiors and any other Christian.

---

[101] Schmaus, M. Pg 188

[102] [102] Dotoohor, A.F., Pg 910.

[103] We observed that during priestly ordination at the Sacred Heart Cathedral Parish, Navrongo-Bolgatanga Diocese on 8th October 2011

Catholic priests are primarily called through baptism to a life of perfection in the same way just as all baptized Christians are called. Priests are obliged to work towards attaining this perfection in a special manner because of their ordination. In affirming this opinion, the Fathers of the Second Vatican Council assert:

> Priests are bound, however, to acquire that perfection in special fashion. They have been consecrated by God in a new manner at their ordination and made living instruments of Christ the Eternal Priest that they may be able to carry on in time his marvelous work whereby the entire family of man is again made whole by power from above. Since, therefore, every priest in his own fashion acts in place of Christ himself, he is enriched by a special grace, so that, as he serves the flock committed to him and the entire People of God, he may the better grow in the grace of him whose tasks he performs, because to the weakness of our flesh there is brought the holiness of him who for us was made a High Priest 'holy, guiltless, undefiled not reckoned among us sinners' (Heb 7:26)[104].

Consequently, Church urges all her priests to make every effort to attain growth in holiness to enable them become "[…] consistently better instruments in the service of the whole people of God, using for this purpose those means which the church has approved".

In spelling out the means to attain perfection in holiness, the Second Vatican Council insists among others on sincerity and indefatigability in attending to priestly duties in "the Spirit of Christ". Priests being ministers of God's word have it as a sacred duty to teach others the Word. Should they be committed to this sincerely and be opened to the Spirit themselves, they would receive the Word first before teaching others. It is the same Word that would make them grow daily and shape them into more perfect followers of the Lord Jesus Christ who called them. Priests act in the person of Christ when offering priestly services, especially in the celebration of the Eucharist, which is a re-enactment of the Christ's sacrifice at Calvary in which he "gave himself for the sanctification of men" (*PO* 13). The Church then requests of her priests "to take example from that with which they deal, and inasmuch as they celebrate the mystery of the Lord's death, they should keep their bodies free of wantonness and lusts"[105].

One outstanding feature that characterizes and distinguishes the life and ministry of the Catholic priest is the Evangelical Counsels; consisting of vows of poverty, chastity and obedience. The Catholic Church demands that the life of her priests should not be marked by affluence and at the same time, the Church does not call her

---

[104] (*PO* 12)

[105] (*PO* 13)

priests into extreme poverty. The Church encourages that as part of their lives priests should not focus on money or be overly indulged in monetary affairs but should only be concerned with what would enable a decent living. In brief, the Church invites all her priests "to embrace voluntary poverty by which they are more manifestly conformed to Christ and become eager in the sacred ministry. For Christ, though he was rich, became poor on account of us, that by his need we might become rich [...]. By living this form of life, priests can laudably reduce to practice that spirit of poverty commended by Christ" [106].

Chastity in the case of the Catholic Church belonging to the Latin rite refers to celibacy. Celibacy is recognized and appreciated by the Church as a gift from God that must be accepted willingly and freely. It was imposed on all who entered into sacred Orders of the Latin Church. Vatican II also approves and confirms celibacy as a priestly way of life. The Council "exhorts all priests who in following the example of Christ freely receive sacred celibacy as a grace of God, that they magnanimously and whole heartedly adhere to it, and that persevering faithfully in it, they may acknowledge this outstanding gift of the Father which is so openly praised and extolled by the Lord (cf Mt 19:11)". Celibacy is suitable for the priestly life as it enables priests to be more committed and dedicated to Christ and his work with undivided heart.

Obedience is very essential in the life of the Catholic priest. Among all the three promises or vows that characterize the priestly life and taken at the diaconate ordination, it is only obedience which is taken again at the priestly ordination. The priest also makes this promise of obedience again to any bishop translated into his diocese. Addai-Mensah encourages the priest "to be true to himself and not contradict by the way he lives what he had publicly sworn [in reference to the promise or vow of obedience] for which people at the ordination ceremony showed their appreciation by their applause"[107]. He again comments that "the vow of obedience is the most difficult" as it confronts the freedom of priests, and their freedom "as human beings in a way through the vow of obedience becomes limited" [108]. The essence of obedience is emphasized by urging priests "[...] to dedicate their own will by obedience to the service of God and their fellow men. In a great spirit of faith, let

---

[106] (*PO* 17)

[107] Addai-Mensah, P.,*Do Diocesan Priests have a Spirituality?: A Ghanaian view*. Takoradi: St Francis Press Ltd, 1997. Pg 37

[108] Addai-Mensah, P. 1997. Pg 37

them receive and execute whatever orders the Holy Father, their own bishop, or other superiors give or recommend"[109].

In addition to their priestly lives, Catholic priests do not live in isolation. As far as they are human, they relate to others. As a relational being, the life of a priest also involves direct relationship with the bishop, fellow priests who are his brothers in ministry and the laity. The Second Vatican Council recommends: "Bishops should regard priests as their brothers and friends and be concerned as far as they are able for their material and especially for their spiritual well-being" (*PO* 7). In view of the recommendation, priests ought to recognize and relate to their bishops as true dependable brothers who would support them both materially and spiritually. In relating to their bishops as recommended, "Priests never losing sight of the fullness of the priesthood which the bishops enjoy, must respect in them the authority of Christ, the supreme shepherd. They must therefore stand by their bishops in sincere charity and obedience" (*PO* 7). The relationship between priests and bishops should be that of mutual respect, dependence and love towards one another and not that of a slave and a master as the Council affirms: "by reason of the gift of the Holy Spirit which is given to priests in Holy Orders, bishops [must] regard them as necessary helpers and counsellors in the ministry and in their role of teaching, sanctifying, nourishing the people of God" (*PO* 7).

Priests are to relate to their fellow priests as brothers because by ordination they are ushered into membership of the Presbyterium of the Catholic Church in which they have other priests as brothers. The Council affirms: "priests by virtue of their ordination to the priesthood are united among themselves in an intimate sacramental brotherhood"[110]. Due to this sacramental brotherhood, it is required of priests to support one another and cooperate effectively in pursuant of "building up the body of Christ" that may require several duties and new methods. The works assigned to various priests may be different yet it should be seen in the broader sense as part of building up the Church of God. Being brothers in the same ministry, priests must offer mutual assistance to develop their intellectual and spiritual life.

Priests who are chosen among the people of God and ordained to minister to the people of God and not angels cannot pursue their ministry without developing a relationship with the laity. Both priests and the laity must develop and maintain a healthy relationship with mutual respect for each other. Priests are spiritual directors and shepherds so they must be available, approachable and accessible to the laity. They must develop and maintain a kind of relationship that would command respect

---

[109] (PO 15)
[110] (PO 8)

nd filial trust from the laity. The relationship between priests and laity should encourage the latter to play her role in the mission of the Church. In view of this, the Fathers of the Second Vatican Council admonish priests to "sincerely acknowledge and promote the dignity of the laity and the part proper to them in the mission of the Church. And they should hold in high honour that just freedom which is due to everyone in the earthly city" [111]. However and fundamentally, priests should recognize that they are brothers to the lay faithful and that they are called to be at the service of their own brothers and sisters; to be with them and not to sit on them.

So far, we have been discussing the life of the Catholic priest without laying much emphasis on his ministry although his life as a priest cannot be separated from his ministry as the latter runs into the former. The discussion from this juncture would lay emphasis on the ministry of the priest. The Catholic priest is committed to the ministry of the Word, Sacraments and a pastoral ministry. The priest is committed to the duty of proclamation of the Word or Gospel to all and sundry.

The priest has the sacred duty to proclaim the Word of salvation through which "the spark of faith is lit in the hearts of unbelievers and fed in the hearts of the faithful" (*PO* 4). The proclamation of the Word may take different forms such as formal preaching during Eucharistic and Para-liturgical celebrations and even the way he lives his life as a priest. The Second Vatican Council observes the importance of the Gospel proclamation and therefore proclaims:

> To all men, therefore, priests are debtors that the truth of the Gospel which they have may be given to others. And so, whether by entering into profitable dialogue they bring people to the worship of God, whether by openly preaching they proclaim the mystery of Christ, or whether in the light of Christ they treat contemporary problems, they are relying not on their own wisdom for it is the word of Christ they teach, and it is to conversion and holiness that they exhort all men [112].

The ministry of the Word prepares the grounds for the Sacramental ministry of the priest. It is only when the Word is proclaimed that people come to faith and would be able to receive the Sacraments. The ministry of the Sacrament strengthens the faithful who are on pilgrimage on this land and draws them closer to God. Vatican II affirms that "By Baptism men are truly brought into the People of God; by the sacrament of Penance sinners are reconciled to God and his Church; by the Anointing of the Sick,

---

[11] (PO 9)

[12] (PO 4)

the ill are given solace; and especially by the celebration of Mass they offer sacramentally the Sacrifice of Christ" [113].

By virtue of ordination, the priest is entrusted with a pastoral ministry as he shares in the office of Christ the shepherd, and head of the Church. In exercising his pastoral ministry, the priest is expected to teach his flock the faith of the Church and ensure that individual members of the flock are led to the Holy Spirit who would enable them live the faith. Living the faith entails not living according to the desires of the self but surrendering the personal will to the demands of the teachings of Christ. Different categories of people make up the flock, the priest is obliged to "treat all with exceptional kindness in imitation of the Lord" and render equal pastoral care for all. It is required of the priest to pay attention to the needs of the youth, married couples and parents. The Fathers of the Second Vatican Council suggest a kind of preferential pastoral care for the poor and the weak in the community. They state, "Although they have obligations toward all men, priests have a special obligation to the poor and weak entrusted to them, for our Lord himself showed that he was united to them, and their evangelization is mentioned as a sign of messianic activity. [...] and above all, priests must be solicitous for the sick and the dying, visiting them and strengthening them in the Lord"[114]. The pastoral ministry of the priest is not limited to the individual care of the faithful but it is extended and culminated in uniting the entire faithful to establish a church that would live in charity with one another and also in unity with the universal Church. This is very crucial and it is lamentable that a priest becomes a principal factor for the division of the Church instead of a unifier.

2.8. Conclusion

The discussion in this chapter has been entirely on the Catholic priesthood with a focus on the historical development, theology, formation of candidates for the priesthood, ordination to the priesthood and life and ministry of the priest. The four major pillars of the priestly formation- human, spiritual, intellectual and pastoral were also discussed. It has been observed that the Catholic priest shares in the priesthood of Christ and acts *in persona Christi* during his ministerial functions. The question now is how do these teachings manifest in the practical and daily life of the priests? To answer the question and many others, in the subsequent chapter, we present the views of priests on areas such as the nature of the priesthood, challenges in the priesthood, and what the Church does to help priests during moments of challenges.

---

[113] (PO 5)

[114] (PO 6)

CHAPTER III

PRESENTATION OF VIEWS OF SOME PRIESTS IN GHANA

3.0. Introduction

In this chapter, we make a presentation and analysis of views shared by some Catholic priests in Ghana. These views may not be much different from those of other priests in other part of the world because of the oneness and universality of the Catholic faith. The major differences that may exist would be in the area of some challenges which may be peculiar to some specific cultural and sociological milieu. These views were obtained within the Catholic Ecclesiastical Provinces of Accra[115], Cape Coast[116] and Kumasi[117].

Questionnaires were used in soliciting for views of the priests for a description of the Catholic priesthood with emphasis on the nature of the priesthood, the call or vocation to the priesthood and challenges in the life and ministry of the priest. Non-probability (quota and purposive) sampling technique was used to select a sample size of four hundred and fifty (450) respondents from the three Ecclesiastical Provinces, with each province assigned with a quota of one hundred and fifty (150). Out of the four hundred and fifty (450) questionnaires distributed, we were able to retrieve three hundred (300) answered questionnaires. Therefore, the total number of respondents was three hundred (300). The answered questionnaires were carefully analysed manually and descriptively.

3.1. Groupings of Respondents

The respondents were divided into five different groups based on the number of years each had served in the priesthood. The first group comprised priests who were not more than five (5) years in the ministry (i.e. the under-five) and they formed the majority with one hundred and twenty (120) representing forty per cent (40%) of the total respondents. The second group was made up of priests who were more than five (5) but less than eleven (11) years in ministry and this represents sixteen per cent (16%) of the respondents i.e. forty-eight (48). The third category of respondents were

---

[115] The Accra Province is made up of the following Dioceses: Accra Archdiocese, Koforidua Diocese, Donkorkrom Vicariate, Ho Diocese, Jasikan Diocese and Keta-Akatsi Diocese.

[116] The Cape Coast Province consists the following: Cape Coast Archdiocese, Sekondi-Takoradi Diocese and Wiawso Diocese.

[117] The Kumasi Province consists the following: Kumasi Archdiocese, Obuasi Diocese, Konongo-Mampong Diocese, Sunyani Diocese, Techiman Diocese, Goaso Diocese

those who had spent eleven years and above but not more than fifteen (15) years in the priesthood and the fourth group was also made up of priests who had been in the priesthood from sixteen (16) up to twenty (20) years. Both the third and fourth group represent twelve per cent (12%) each i.e. thirty-six (36) respondents for each group. The fifth category was made up of respondents who had been in the priesthood for twenty one (21) years and above and they were sixty (60) representing twenty per cent (20%). The groupings enabled us to identify and appreciate some challenges that were peculiar to a specific group of priests.

3.2. Nature of the Catholic Priesthood

All the three hundred (300) respondents, representing hundred per cent (100%) answering question on the nature of the priesthood emphasized that the priesthood is of service in nature. The key word in the priesthood is "service" and priests are to serve in whatever capacity the Church places them. It is also in accordance with the assertion of Burghardt that priests are to render service to humanity[118]. Out of the total percentage (100%), ten per cent (10%) representing thirty (30) respondents also added that the Catholic priesthood is celibate and male oriented in nature because of ecclesiastical discipline rather than theology. For these thirty (30); celibacy is not to be seen as coming from God, but principally it is the church's imposition, nothing theological and therefore not evangelical. Even though it is not celibacy that makes one a Catholic priest, nevertheless, it still is and remains one of the visible and distinctive features of the Catholic priesthood in the Latin rite.

From the various answers provided by the respondents, we deduce that the Catholic priesthood is an answer to a divine call to participate in the priesthood of Jesus Christ through the ministry of the Church. The priest by his ordination is configured to Christ or becomes *alter Christus* and acts in *persona Christi*. The priest is called to serve the people of God through total surrender of his life to God for the salvation of souls.

3.3. The Call to the Priesthood

The views expressed by the priests affirmed that the call to which the priest answers is a strong and irresistible desire to embrace the priestly ministry in spite of the challenges and difficulties involved. A genuine call stems out of extreme love for God and desire to be used by God to serve humanity in that state of life. A genuine

---

[118] Burrghardt, W.J. 1981. Pg 168

call would lead to an interest in the priesthood while an interest may not necessarily lead to a call. An interest in the priesthood alone cannot constitute a call, as the former may be a mere admiration for the ministry due to ones encounter with a priest. The interest may also be because of the perceived seemingly "good living" and respect that priests enjoy.

Two hundred and sixteen (216) of the respondents, representing seventy two per cent (72%) claimed that they received a genuine call that later generated an interest in them while eighty-four (84); representing twenty eight per cent (28%) of priests interviewed claimed that their desire to be priests was both a call and an interest at the same time. The respondents realized their call to the priesthood at various stages of their lives. Twenty-four (24) representing eight per cent (8%) had their call before teenage, one hundred and fifty-six (156), representing fifty two per cent (52%) at adolescence and one hundred and twenty (120), representing forty per cent (40%) became conscious of their call at adulthood (this includes students in the tertiary institutions, people learning trade, workers and the unemployed). One significant deduction from the above is that God calls people into the ministry of the priesthood at all stages of life and the call cannot be limited to a specific stage.

According to our findings, the call to the priesthood may take several forms. Some may be dramatic while others may take ordinary forms. Twenty-four (24) of the respondents, representing eight per cent (8%) claimed to have been called through persistent dreams; another eight per cent (8%) heard an unknown voice admonishing them to serve God as priests, twelve (12) representing four per cent (4%) were called through the serene Seminary environment while they were on visit, thirty-six (36) representing twelve per cent (12%) received their call as a result of inspiration and good exemplary lives of their parish priests; one hundred and eight (108) representing thirty-six per cent (36%) felt called while they were very actively participating in church activities and even serving on the youth council while ninety-six (96) representing thirty-two per cent (32%) felt called through their services as altar boys or Mass servers.

The individual priests reacted differently when they became conscious of their calling into the sacred priesthood. Two hundred and four (204) of the respondents representing sixty-eight per cent (68%) claimed to have willingly accepted the call with excitement and prayer, while ninety-six (96) representing thirty-two per cent (32%) were hesitant from the initial stages but with prayer, they were able to accept the call. According to one hundred and ninety-two (192) representing sixty-four per cent (64%) of the respondents, their family offered them full support in their decision to be priests Ninety six (96) representing thirty-two per cent (32%) had a mixed reaction from family as some members were in support of the decision and others opposed it. Twelve (12) respondents representing four per cent (4%) also claimed that they had total opposition from the entire family and this continued even during their Seminary formation but the family hesitantly gave in at the time of ordination.

In answering a question to find out the possibility of refusing the call to the priesthood and its consequence, one hundred and eight (108) representing thirty-six per cent (36%) of the priests interviewed responded negatively, with the reason that no one can refuse a divine call simply because God initiates it. One hundred and ninety-two (192) representing sixty-four per cent (64%) of the respondents were also of the view that they could have said no to the call but the consequences would have been unfulfillment in life.

3.4. Challenges in the Catholic Priesthood

After accepting the call and going through formation, the candidate is ordained into the priesthood, and then begins the life and ministry of priests. The life and ministry of a Catholic priest also comes along with its own challenges. The respondents identified challenges in the priesthood as the daily struggles, obstacles and difficulties that characterize the priestly life and ministry. All respondents representing hundred per cent (100%) said they have all gone through one challenge or the other in their priestly ministry.

In listing some of the challenges in the priesthood, the evangelical counsels namely: obedience, celibacy/chastity and poverty appeared to have been the commonest challenge to all the groups of the respondents, followed by stress and the negative attitude of some parishioners. About two hundred and seventy (270) representing ninety per cent (90%) of the respondents listed obedience to God through their bishops/superiors, parish priests and older priests as a challenge. For them it is very difficult to obey and discern the will of God through obedience to authority or superiors. Still in connection with obedience, respondents see it as a great challenge to maintain appropriate relationship with authority without showing signs of disobedience. For most respondents to identify obedience as one of their challenges confirms the assertion of Addai-Mensah that "the vow of obedience is the most difficult"[119] as it limits the freedom of priests as full mature human beings.

Two hundred and ten (210) representing seventy per cent (70%) of the respondents also included loving their state of poverty as a challenge. For them, poverty becomes

---

[119] Addai-Mensah, P. Pg 37

challenge because of the pressure put on them by their respective families to make financial contributions. According to them in times of financial difficulties, members of their families demand financial support from them, especially to pay school fees, health bills, contribution towards family funerals and even money to start a trade. One hundred and ninety-two (192) representing sixty-four per cent (64%) of the respondents also included chastity as a challenge. For them chastity is equivalent to priestly celibacy and should always begin from the mind, it is a challenge to always make the conscious effort to keep the mind pure regardless of what the eyes may see. Ninety (90) representing thirty per cent (30%) of the respondents expressed the view that Protestantism and specifically extreme Pentecostalism was a challenge in the sense that some youthful parishioners expect their priests to carry out the priestly work in such extreme Pentecostal fashion which may even be contrary to Catholic spirituality.

One hundred and sixty two (162) representing fifty-four (54%) of the respondents confirmed that stress is another challenge in their ministry. About one hundred fifty (150), representing fifty per cent (50%) of the respondents also included in the list of challenges, the attitude of some parishioners that appear to be unacceptable such as gossiping and peddling of falsehood about priests, yet the priest must maintain appropriate relationship with them.

Eighty-four (84) representing seventy per cent (70%) of the respondents who had been in the priesthood for not more than five (5) years shared that the ability to maintain healthy relationship with the opposite sex without any emotional attachments is a challenge. There are also two peculiar challenges to priests who have been in ministry for twenty-one (21) years and above. Forty-two (42) representing seventy per cent (70%) of such priests saw it as a challenge to keep up with their prayer and spiritual life with emphasis on being faithful to the praying of the Office of the Hours. The same percentage (70%) of respondents thought of it as a challenge to correct some of the long held, but erroneous opinions that some parishioners have concerning the Church, such as the Church belongs to the clergy and not recognizing that the Church, which is a family of God, both the laity and clergy are brothers and sisters and each has his/her specific role to play for the growth of the church.

The ability of priests to rise above their various challenges strengthens them and makes them faithful to their ministry. All respondents shared that in attempts to overcome their challenges, they develop a hopeful attitude towards the challenge, resort to prayer and counseling and take other pragmatic steps based on the particular challenge. Two hundred and seventy (270) representing ninety per cent (90%) of the respondents said that the Church continues to help priests to overcome challenges through on-going formation, regular retreats and recollections and those with extreme challenges are sent to rehabilitation centres which are manned by the Church for assistance.

In spite of all the challenges associated with the priesthood, two hundred and eighty-eight (288) representing ninety-six per cent (96%) of the respondents said they do not regret being in that vocation while twelve (12), representing four per cent (4%) also said they sometimes regret but the feeling of regret does not last long. They emphasized that they experience the feelings of regret when their family members are in dire need of money and they as priests are incapable of contributing to redeem them from such helpless situations.

3.5. Conclusion

So far, we deduce from the views expressed by these active priests that, the priesthood is a divine call to serve God and humanity by participating in the priesthood of Jesus Christ through the ministry of the church. Those who become priests receive their specific call at various stages of their lives. Also, the priesthood demands a daily response from the priest to his calling. The vow of obedience also stands out as the most common challenge to all priests. In the next chapter, the study would be on the notion of priesthood from some other religious perspectives.

CHAPTER IV

A BIBLICAL SURVEY ON CATHOLIC PRIESTHOOD

4.0. Introduction

This chapter is to elucidate the foundation of ministerial priesthood through a biblical survey. The discussion would be from the Old and New Testament perspectives.

4.1. Priesthood in the Old Testament (OT)

D.M. McFarlan explains priest in the OT as a man who was "specially set apart for the duties of animal sacrifice and other religious rites in the tabernacle or local shrine and later in the Temple of Jerusalem"[120]. From the *Encyclopaedia Judaica,* "Priests are the principal functionaries in divine services, their special task being to engage in cultic ceremonies which they conducted mainly in the Temple"[121]. The priest therefore was the link between the worshipper and God. He served as the bridge across the people and Yahweh. During the OT period, the patriarchs performed what could be regarded specifically as priestly functions although they never applied the term to themselves. For instance; Noah erected an altar and offered sacrifice to the Lord (Gen 8:20-21), Abraham offered a ram as burnt offering in place of his promised son Isaac (Gen 22: 1-14) and Jacob killed an animal and offered it as a sacrifice (Gen 31:54). These few examples show that no explicit connection existed between sacrifice and priesthood in the patriarchal period. There was also no clear definition of the priesthood and it was not an exclusively reserved duty of a specific tribe as it became later.

However, Abraham during his lifetime encountered the mysterious Melchizedek who is identified to be a king and a priest of the Most High God (Gen 14:18-20). Melchizedek offered the sacrifice of bread and wine while Abraham gave him one tenth of the spoils accrued from his military expedition. Melchizedek received Abraham's offering not as a result of royalty but the former being a priest as we can recognize in the later well-organized Israel, one tenth was offered to the Levitical priests and not the kings. It is significant to point out clearly that Melchizedek's priesthood has no link with the later Levitical priesthood and Melchizedek's

---

[120] McFarlan, D.M. *Dictionary of the Bible.* (New Lanark: Geddes & Grosset, 2003), 220.

[121] *Encyclopaedia Judaica.* (Jerusalem: Keter Publishing House Jerusalem Ltd, 1972), 1069.

47

priesthood cannot be used to argue for the existence of a particular priesthood at the patriarchal period.

Again, there could not have been an organized priesthood under the leadership of Aaron or his sons immediately after the exodus from Egypt. Although Moses was never called a priest in the Pentateuch, there are some traditions that present "Moses performing 'priestly' acts: he appears, to 'preside' at Aaron's 'ordination' and to manipulate the sacrificial blood at the liturgy which follows (see Ex 29)"[122].

 In the history of Israel, Moses mediated between God and the people, and transmitted messages he received from Yahweh to the people. In agreement with N. Mitchell, Moses played the role of a priest in the transition period between the exodus from Egypt and the beginnings of Hebrew settlement in Canaan. At a point in time in the Jewish history, emerged a defined priestly office to which some men devoted their whole time. R.E. Brown argues that this emergence was due to growth in the social organization of Israel, leading to the development of professional priesthood in connection with the tribe of Levi. The professional prowess of the Levites culminated exclusively in the Levitical priesthood[123].

Several scholars do advance different hypotheses about the origin and emergence of the Levites as a class of professional priests. However, N. Mitchell cites that of Aelred Cody to be the most convincing. He suggests that in Cody's hypothesis, the exact origin of the tribe of Levi is unknown and therefore assumes that it was a full secular tribe such as Reuben, Dan etc. For unknown reasons the Levites could not acquire land during the tribal settlement in Palestine. The members of the tribe took residence among members of the other tribes, although they were all "people of the same racial stock […] [they] were not members of the tribe among whom they lived". The Levites then took to specializing in "priestly jobs such as priestly attendants and oracular consultants"[124]. Therefore, D.M. McFarlan posits that traditionally all priests were to be descendants of Levi. A descendant of Levi becomes a priest because he has been born into such a priestly tribe[125]. Further affirmation is placed on this explication by other authors including N. Mitchell that the position of the Levitical priest was not acquired through any ritual act, rather, the Levite assumed his position

---

[122] Mitchell, N. *Mission and Ministry: History and Theology in the Sacrament of Order.* (Wilmington, Delaware: Michael Glazier, 1982), 24.

[123] Brown, R.E., *Priest and Bishop: Biblical reflections.* (New York: Paulist Press, 1970), 6.

[124] Mitchell, N. *Mission and Ministry: History and Theology in the Sacrament of Order*, 27.

[125] McFarlan, D.M. *Dictionary of the Bible*, 220.

by exercising priestly functions. The Levitical priesthood was more of a craft than a "sacred office" or "divine vocation"[126].

For R.E. Brown, the Levitical priest entered into that ministry by virtue of his birth. He became a priest because of being a member of the priestly tribe. His calling by God to that priesthood should only be regarded in terms of "divine providence guiding his birth"[127]. The Levites guarded jealously their status perhaps because "the tribe had no land to serve as economic base of operations"[128]. Nevertheless, not all Levites became priests and not all priests were Levites. For instance, Zadok who was initially not linked with Levi became a priest in the house of David during the latter's reign, and later his descendants also claimed priestly rights and were referred to as Zadokites. They also served as priests when Solomon became king. Some Levitical priests were descendants of Zadok (Ezekiel 44:15) and it suggests a relationship between the Levites and Zadokites. In support of this, N. Mitchell affirms that in the "restored post-exilic community" both Levites and Zadokites traced their ancestry to Aaron[129]. Moses and Aaron are listed among the descendants of Levi (Exodus 6:14-27). The Zadokites claimed supremacy over the Levitical priests and this could be as a result of Ezekiel 44:6ff that God reduced the priestly status of the Levites as they were unreliable in their care of the sanctuary and due to Aaron's role in the Israelites rebellion at Merribah. God transferred the priesthood to Eleazar who is a son of Aaron (Num 20:24-29) and in 1 Chronicles 6:50-53, he is presented as a direct ancestor of Zadok. In the post-exilic Jewish community, the priests whether Levites or Zadokites, were cultic functionaries endowed with the responsibility of attending to daily sacrifices, while the high priest was not obliged to attend to such daily sacrifices. His obligatory day was the annual Day of Atonement during which he offered sin offerings of bull and goats for the priests' transgressions, sprinkled blood and burnt incense in the Holy of Holies for atonement of sin, and performed the rites of purification, which also involved sprinkling of blood at the altar in the sanctuary.

One remarkable characteristic of the Old Testament priesthood, be it a Levite or Zadokite, is that it was not devoid of sanctity. The priest was made holy for the purpose of his office and by the office itself. Yahweh commanded all Israel to be holy as He is holy (Lev 19:2) and this placed a greater demand of holiness on the priest as he mediated between God and the people. It is affirmed that "the priests being essentially servants of God enjoy greater holiness than the rest of the people

---

126 Mitchell, N. *Mission and Ministry: History and Theology in the Sacrament of Order*, 28.

127 Brown, R.E., *Priest and Bishop: Biblical reflections*, 7.

128 Mitchell, N. *Mission and Ministry: History and Theology in the Sacrament of Order*, 28.

129 Mitchell, N. *Mission and Ministry: History and Theology in the Sacrament of Order*, 43.

[…] the holiness of the priests equals the holiness of the house of God itself". There were several external signs that affirmed the "identification of the priests with the holiness of the house of God"[130]. Purity was demanded from the priest in all his endeavours but greater purity was demanded during his priestly duties. In maintaining the purity attached to the priesthood, the priests were subjected to special obligations and restrictions.

The primary function of the priest in the Old Testament was the performance of sacrifice. The priest had an outstanding duty to offer sacrifices on the altar that stood on the Temple court. This particular function of the priest can be classified into two major roles: sprinkling the blood and burning portions of the sacrifices. The ordinary priests performed these functions daily while "the high priest was entrusted with the sin offerings, especially that of the Day of Atonement". Besides the offering of sacrifices the priests were also in charge of maintenance of the Temple. They carried out routine inspections on the Temple grounds to identify what needed to be repaired and solicited funds to carry out such repair works. In addition, the priests performed purification rites for those who suffered diseases or physical impurity. Also, it was the duty of the priests to diagnose the disease and purify the victims and objects affected by such impurity. The methods of purification rites involved the victim waiting for a specific time, taking a bath, washing clothes and items used during the period of disease or impurity, and offering of sacrifice[131].

R. E. Brown observes two additional functions of priests and these are the consultation of the *Urim and Thummim* at the sanctuary and a teaching function. The consultation of *Urim and Thummim* refers to the casting of sacred lots to help identify God's will in a particular situation. For instance; Moses decreed that the Lord would reveal His will to the Levitical priests through *Urim and Thummin* (Deut. 33:8)[132]. The priests gradually lost the performance of this sacred function to the prophets during the monarchical period. The priests of the Old Testament also served as teachers. The function of teaching is ascribed to the priests in Deuteronomy 33:10. As priests, they were the teachers of the *Torah*. The function of giving instruction concerning the *Torah* although did not exist as a special established institution, was part of their everyday activities. For instance, the instruction and guidance given in matters of impurities and diseases were all aspect of teaching the *Torah*. From the

---

[130] *Encyclopaedia Judaica*, 1080.

[131] Achtemeier, P.J. (Gen. Ed.). *Harper's Bible Dictionary*. (Bangalore: Theological Publications, 1990).

[132] Brown, R.E., *Priest and Bishop: Biblical reflections*, 10.

bove, priesthood was a religious institution that emerged and developed gradually during the Jewish settlement in Palestine after the exodus from Egypt.

.2. Priesthood in the New Testament (NT)

3. Gleeson espouses that a thorough study of ministry from the NT shows the impossibility of enumerating the exact ministries that existed[133]. The focus is on the presbyterate, however, it cannot be discussed in isolation, so the discussion shall commence with the ministries of the episcopate and diaconate, before narrowing it down to the focus of study in this chapter. J. Macquarrie asserts that "in the first few centuries, throughout the whole Church, the various kinds of ministry of which we read in the New Testament had become consolidated into the familiar three orders of bishops, priests and deacons". He further illuminates that "the bishops were thought of as the successors of the apostles, who were supposed to have founded [...] the principal sees of the ancient Church; the priests (or presbyters) corresponded to the pastors indifferently called 'bishops' or 'presbyters' in the New Testament; while the deacons represented those inferior orders of ministry which we can also see in the New Testament"[134]. The idea of the bishops being the successors of the apostles is more of tradition than any biblical evidence.

"Bishop" is translated from the Greek *episkopos*, which means "overseer", the bishop, therefore is an overseer of God's flock. The bishop ought to be wholesome and exhibit if not all, most of the qualities that Paul enumerated in his letters (1 Tim 3:1-8; Titus 1:6-9). For P. Toon, the title "bishop" was used to describe "the function of the presbyter (elder)" during the NT period[135]. The implication of his opinion is a lack of clear distinction between the bishop and the presbyter; the latter could be referred to as bishop due to his functions. The bishop is a presbyter who presides over gatherings of presbyters.

In his contribution to the issue of any distinction between presbyters and bishops, Josef Ratzinger postulates that, Jewish Christian leaders were referred to as presbyters while the leaders of the Gentile churches were referred to as "bishops and deacons" for the first time in Philippians 1:1. This postulation assumes no clear distinction between the two. In affirmation with J.L. McKenzie, there is no clear

---

[33] Gleeson, B., Ordained Persons and their Ministries: New Testament Foundations and Variations. *Australian*

[34] Macquarrie, J., *Principles of Christian Theology*. 2nd ed. (New York: Charles Scribner's Sons, 1977), 431.

[35] Toon, P. "Bishop". In: *Evangelical Dictionary of Theology*, 2nd ed. (Michigan: Baker Academic, 2001), 170.

distinction between the bishop and the presbyter as there is between the former and the deacon[136].

Some theologians such as J.Macquarrie are of the view that the diaconate is the least among the three clearly defined special ministries in the NT and recognize its prototype in the ministry of Stephen and his companions[137] (Acts 6:1-7). G.M. Burge also traces the beginning of the diaconate to the appointment of the seven whose primary duty was to help with the distribution of food in order for the apostles to continue effectively with preaching[138]. However, they were not limited to this as Stephen was noted for performing great signs and wonders (Acts 6:8) which led to his martyrdom; Philip was also a missionary who preached to and baptized an Ethiopian eunuch (Acts 8:26-40). Although the seven were called to service, Luke does not refer to the seven as "deacons" although tradition ascribes the institution of the diaconate to the choice of the seven[139]. From the Jerusalem Church, the diaconate spread to the Gentile churches.

Many authors including R.S. Wallace associate the presbyterate to the beginning of the church, "taking their place along with the apostles, prophets, and teachers". He identifies the presbyterate at Jerusalem with James in "the government of the local church after the manner of the synagogue (Acts 11:3; 21:18)"[140]. B. Gleeson affirms that the presbyterate was "a form of leadership in Jewish synagogues (Acts 15:22) and practiced by the first Christians, who were themselves Jews"[141]. The presbyters functioned as overseers in the absence of apostles and essentially as teachers and preachers (1 Tim 5:17). The kind of presbyterate practiced by the first Century Christians should not be thought of as today's priests even though the Second Vatican Council referred to the latter as presbyterate. The presbyterate in the Catholic sense is associated with sacerdotalism and for that matter her priesthood is in essence of the term, although the NT does not apply the term "priest" to any single person. With the exception of the priest of Zeus (Acts 14:13); any reference to priests and high priest

---

[136] McKenzie, J.L. *Dictionary of the Bible*. (London: Cassell Publishers Limited, 1968), 97.

[137] Macquarrie, J., *Principles of Christian Theology*. 2nd ed, 432, 433.

[138] Burge, G.M. "Deacon, Deaconess". In: *Evangelical Dictionary of Theology*, 2nd ed. (Michigan: Baker Academic, 2001), 320.

[139] Dunn, P.J. *Priesthood: A Re-examination of the Roman Catholic theology of the Presbyterate*. (New York: Alba House, 1990), 50.

[140] Wallace, R.S., "Elder". In: *Evangelical Dictionary of Theology*, 2nd ed. (Michigan: Baker Academic, 2001), 369.

[141] Gleeson, B., Ordained Persons and their Ministries: New Testament Foundations and Variations. *Australian*

in the Gospels and Acts "assume an historical and religious continuity with the Old Testament"[142] .

The Christian community is commissioned as a "royal priesthood" and "holy nation" (1 Peter 2:5, 9; Rev 1:6) by virtue of baptism, making them participants in the priesthood of Christ. The concept of a "royal priesthood" and "holy nation" is not peculiar to Christians, because in the Old Testament, God referred to the Jews as "a priestly kingdom and holy nation" (Exodus 19:6) and it did not conflict or prevent in anyway the emergence of the Jewish priesthood.

The early Christians recognized the Jewish priesthood as valid and therefore did not conceive of theirs. According to R.E. Brown, the Christian community thought of herself as "a movement within Judaism differing only in some features (especially in the belief that Jesus was the Messiah, that with him God had inaugurated the eschatological times, and [...] Gentiles could now participate fully in the blessings of Israel without formally adopting all the precepts of the Law of Moses)"[143]. The Christians identified themselves as the "renewed Israel" and were in anticipation that all Israel would soon join the "renewal movement". Luke accounts that Jerusalem Christians continued their daily attendance to the Temple although they were also gathering to break bread in their homes (Acts 2:46). Paul also continued to go to the Temple and in some cases participated in offerings (Acts 21:26).

J. Martos and others affirm that the early Christians, who were mostly Jews, accepted the validity of the Jewish priesthood, and showed this by continuous worship at the temple until its destruction in AD 70 by Roman soldiers30. These prove that the early Christians did not reject the Jewish priesthood from the initial stages, so they did not see the need for the development of their own form of priesthood. Some Christians began to identify themselves not just as a movement, but a new religion different from Judaism and a replacement of the Jews as "God's covenanted people". Others also interpreted the destruction of the Jewish Temple as God's rejection of the Jews due to their failure to acknowledge Jesus as the Messiah. As a result, the concept of "special Christian priesthood" in place of the Jewish priesthood gradually emerged due partly to the above reasons. Such a development of priesthood is assigned in the letter to the Hebrews.

---

[142] Wood, D.R.W. (Gen. Ed.). *New Bible Dictionary*. 3rd Ed. (Nottingham: Inter-Varsity Press, 1996), 960.

[143] Brown, R.E., *Priest and Bishop: Biblical reflections*, 17.

The most striking theme in the letter to the Hebrews is the prominent presentation of Jesus as an eternal *archiereus* (high priest). This may be surprising because the historical Jesus was not a priest and appears to have been a critic of the temple practices and was at odds with the Jerusalem priesthood (Mk 11:15-18). The author defends his presentation of Jesus as *hiereus* (priest) by appealing to the mysterious figure of Melchizedek (Gen 14:18-20), who is identified as a priest long before the institution of the Levitical priesthood. Jesus' priesthood is presented in the order of Melchizedek (Heb 5:6, 10; 6:20; 7:17).

M.   A. Powell observes "that neither the genealogy nor the death of Melchizedek reported in the Bible indicates [...] the superior priesthood that he represents [...], having neither beginning nor end"[144]. The priesthood of Jesus Christ is an element of the new and better covenant of which he is the mediator by virtue of embracing death by the cross. He is the only mediator because his sacrifice is the means of reconciliation between God and human beings. It has taken away sin, which is the obstacle to the relationship between God and humanity and restored the relationship. M.M. Bourke affirms that the superiority of the new covenant to the old is based on the eternity of its priesthood that is in Jesus Christ.

The author of the letter to the Hebrews emphasises that Jesus is a royal priest, whose death has been the ultimate sacrifice that had rendered continuation of animal sacrifice ineffective. He also presents Christianity as a perfect replacement of the old Israel[145]. Christians then took on the identity of the new Israel. As the new Israel, Christians needed to replace the Jewish bloody sacrifice. It is in this context that R.E. Brown asserts that "the Eucharist was seen as unbloody sacrifice replacing the bloody sacrifices no longer offered in the now-destroyed Temple". He posited that, as early as the end of the first century, Christians had identified the Eucharist as a sacrifice. He affirms his position with *Didache* 14: "Assemble on the Lord's Day, breaking bread and celebrating the Eucharist; but first confess your sins that your sacrifice [*thysia*] may be a pure one... for it was of this that the Lord spoke"[146] .

Acknowledging the Eucharist as sacrifice meant that whoever presided over it then functioned as priest and it contributed to the emergence of a ministerial priesthood. The Catholic priesthood therefore became associated with the celebration of the

---

[144] Powell, M.A. *Introducing the New Testament: A Historical, Literary and Theological Survey.* (Michigan: Baker Academic, 2009), 438.

[145] Bourke, M.M., The Epistle to the Hebrews. *The New Jerome Biblical Commentary.* (London: Burns and Oates, 1995).

[146] Brown, R.E., *Priest and Bishop: Biblical reflections*, 19.

Eucharist which is the unbloody sacrifice that has replaced the bloody sacrifice, offered once and for all by Jesus Christ the eternal high priest. Whenever the Eucharistic sacrifice is celebrated, it is the re-enactments of the actual sacrifice that Jesus offered in which he was both the victim and the priest.

4.3. Conclusion

The discussion in this chapter has been on the biblical foundations of ministerial priesthood. It has been traced from the patriarchal period through the exodus to the settling in Palestine and the rise of the Levitical priesthood. We deduce from the New Testament that the term "priest" did not apply to a single person but the entire Christian community. The early Christian community also accepted the Jewish priesthood until Christians realized their identity as the "new Israel" and accepted the Eucharist as a replacement of the Jewish bloody sacrifice leading to the emergence of a ministerial priesthood to which corresponds the Catholic priesthood which is realistic priesthood in essence.

CHAPTER V

THE NOTION OF PRIESTHOOD FROM SOME OTHER RELIGIOUS PERSPECTIVES IN GHANA

5.0. Introduction

We have already noted in the introductory chapter that Ghana is a religiously pluralistic society with an official recognition of three main religions – African Traditional Religion, Islam and Christianity. There are countless denominations within the Protestant tradition of Christianity. All these religious groups or and denominations have their equivalent to the Catholic priest. The focus of the discussion would be on the parallels of the Catholic priesthood in the African Traditional Religion and with emphasis from the Akan perspective, some mainline churches within the Protestant tradition and the African Indigenous Churches (AICs). The parallel of the Catholic priesthood in Protestant tradition is a clerical ministry (pastoral) or representative priesthood.

5.1. Priesthood in African Traditional Religions

In African traditional religions, the priest can be a man, woman called by the gods, trained and dedicated to a particular public or family shrine or sacred grove for ritual purposes in the interests of the community he, or she serves. Ekwunife describes a traditional priest as "someone summoned either by the divinity or by his community or by some form of religious impulse to fulfil a religious function for the salvation of the community or for self-devotion"[147].

According to African scholars such as Mbiti[148], Opoku[149] and Quarcoopome[150], priests in traditional African set up, are essentially the chief intermediaries; they stand between man, God and or other divinities associated with the African worldview especially in sacrificial matters. The priest's essential role in African society is quite different from the roles of other specialists of African Traditional Religion like kings, queens, diviners, mediums, prophets and rain makers, to mention but a few. The

---

[147] Ekwunife, A.N.O., 1999. The Priesthood in African Traditional Religion. *Bigard Theological Studies*, 19 (1), Pg 26

[148] Mbiti, J.S. *African Religions & Philosophy*. London: Heinemann,1969. Pg 68

[149] Opoku, K.A. *West African Traditional Religion*. Accra: FEP International Private Limited, 1978. Pg 74

[150]Quarcoopome, T.N.O. *West African Traditional Religion*. Ibadan: African Universities Press, 1987. Pg 77

ssential role of the priest in sacrificial affairs does not mean that the other specialists noted above do not offer ritual sacrifice on behalf of the community or on their clients. In offering ritual sacrifices, they perform priestly functions although they are not recognized as priests. In support of this, Mbiti notes that the Baganda king used to make an offering and sacrifice of nine men, nine women, nine cattle, nine goats, nine fowls, and nine loads of bark cloths and cowry shells[151]. Ekwunife also observes that the *Asantehene* who occupies the golden stool is by virtue of his position the main presider of ritual offerings and sacrifices during the *Adae* festival[152].

There are two types of priesthood in the African society; Quarcoopome categorizes them into lay and professional priesthood. Those who make up the lay priesthood are the family or clan heads who officiate at the domestic and ancestral shrines where they lead the household in making offerings and prayers. Those who belong to the professional priesthood are those connected to the cult of the divinities. The Yoruba of Nigeria refer to them as *Olorisha* while they are known as *Akomfo* among the Akans of Ghana[153]. These professional priests are set aside from birth to dedicate their lives to the priesthood by virtue of inheritance from any of the parents or a relative. The candidates for the professional priesthood may also be chosen through the medium of spirit possession. In the latter, the spirit of a divinity may possess a person of his choice and the one chosen may be secluded from the public for training for a period, depending on the divinity. The period ranges from three weeks to three years or more. The choice of a divinity for the priesthood is formally trained in the art of the priesthood at the traditional centres for training priests and priestesses. At the end of the training, the candidate for the sacred office goes through the rite of initiation into the priesthood[154].

The African traditional priest is a significant religious and social figure due to the essential roles he or she plays in the community. Mbiti posits that as an intermediary, the priest is also the religious symbol of God and the divinities among the people. He speaks and understands the language of the divine so he is expected to translate and interpret this language to the people whenever the need arises. The priest also performs ritual sacrifices and offerings on behalf of the community. For instance, when there are national disasters such as plagues, death, famine and drought, to mention a few, the priest offers the required sacrifice to God, the ancestors and the other divinities concerned[155].

---

[151] Mbiti, J.S. 1969. Pg 188
[152] Ekwunife, A.N.O., 1999. Pg 11
[153] Quarcoopome, T.N.O. 1987. Pg 74
[154] Quarcoopome, T.N.O. 1987. Pg 76
[155] Mbiti, J.S. 1969. Pg 188

The traditional priest is also an important social figure because after his priestly training he becomes the custodian of societal or communal customs, knowledge and wisdom, taboos and the history of the society. In support of this view, Opoku affirms, "priests are [...] repositories of communal knowledge and traditions" [156]. The privileged position of the priest makes him an advisor to the chief or king and a ritual expert. The traditional priest together with the chief is the custodian of the traditions and culture of the community. He sees to it that the inhabitants of the community adhere to the traditional norms and culture of the land. The priest also assumes the position of a judge in some instances such as managing and resolving conflicts that involve witchcraft accusations and curses. He administers oath for restoring confidence in a community or adjudicating justice on the offended party. He is also recognized as an opinion leader. He is primarily a presider over rituals and this earns him the position of an elder in the traditional community. We have seen the concept of priesthood from African indigenous perspective; we would now examine the concept from Christian perspective with our focus on the Protestant tradition.

5.2. Christian Priesthood

Christian priesthood or Christian ministry is a particular reference to the clergy who are set apart by virtue of ordination or commissioning in the various Christian traditions to preach the gospel, administer sacraments and perform other pastoral functions [157]. The various Christian denominations have different titles for the ordained or the commissioned representatives who perform clerical functions. We have already observed that in the Catholic tradition, such persons are solely males referred to as priests in the essence of the term. However, in the Protestant tradition they are both males and females referred to as pastors or ministers, and in some African Independent Churches within the same Protestant tradition, they are referred to as priests or prophets/prophetesses. The synonymous use of the terms priest and minister in this chapter would be in reference to the clergy or the ordained persons.

5.3. The Protestant Ministry

It is important to note that almost all Protestant churches hold similar or even the same view on priesthood or the ordained ministry with exception to the Anglican Church that shares the same view with the Catholic Church. We now turn our attention to some of the churches in Ghana that can be identified with the Protestant

---

[156] Opoku, K.A. 1978. Pg 74
[157] Ekem, JDK. 2009. Pg 101

tradition, namely: the Presbyterian Church and the Methodist Church. We are focusing on these churches from the Protestant tradition because they are the largest, vibrant and well-organized mainline Protestant churches in Ghana.

5.3.1. The Presbyterian Ministry

The concept of the ordained ministry in the Presbyterian Church of Ghana has its roots in the concept of ministry introduced by the Basel Evangelical Missionary Society. Ekem affirms that the concept is also a reflection of the comprehension of ministry that was upheld during the Protestant Reformation. The Protestant Reformers laid emphasis on the common priesthood of all believers that is attained by the individual in the reception of the Sacrament of Baptism. They were also quick to admit the existence of "representative priesthood" which is not superior to the common priesthood of all believers and does not require any sacerdotal function[158].

Ekem again posits that those who are called into the ordained ministry of the Presbyterian Church in Ghana are representative priests who stand as "servants or ministers of God in relation to the *ecclesia Dei*, ministers of the Word and Sacraments rather than priestly mediators in the Roman Catholic sense of the word"[159]. The Presbyterian ordained ministry falls within the category of presbyters who have it as their duty to preach the Word and also to administer the Sacraments. The concept of ministry embraced by the Presbyterian Church is not different from that of the Methodist Church; both churches hold the same foundational beliefs concerning the ministry. We now turn to the concept of the ministry in the Methodist Church, Ghana.

5.3.2. The Methodist Ministry

Concerning the concept of priesthood/ordained ministry in the Methodist Church, the constitution of the Methodist Church states:

> Christ's Ministers in the church are stewards in the household of God and shepherds of his flock. Some are called and ordained to this sole occupation and have a principal and directing part in these duties, but they hold no priesthood differing in kind from that which is common to the Lord's people and they have no exclusive title to the preaching of the

---

[158] Ekem, JDK. 2009. Pg 102

[159] Ekem, JDK. 2009. Pg 103

gospel or the care of the souls. Others, to whom also the Spirit divides His gifts as he wills, share these ministries with them. (S.O. 4 (1)) [...]

[Furthermore] the Methodist Church holds the doctrine of priesthood of all believers, and consequently believes that no priesthood exists which belongs exclusively to a particular order or class of persons; but in the exercise of its corporate life and worship, special qualifications for the discharge of special duties are required, and thus the principle of representative selection is recognized (S.O. 4 (4)).[160]

The Methodist Church recognizes some people as "called of God", gives them a theological formation in a seminary and ordains such people into her ministry. The ordination symbolizes the church's recognition of the "minister's personal call". The ordination also sets the minister apart to proclaim the Word and to administer the Sacraments. It is well enshrined in the Methodist constitution that, "[...] for the sake of Church Order and not because of any priestly virtue inherent in the office [of the ordained minister], the Ministers of the Methodist Church are set apart by ordination"[161]. The ordained ministry is not a priestly ministry and for that matter, the minister does not perform any exclusive priestly function. The only recognized priesthood is that of all believers which includes both the minister and the laity. The ministers and lay people in the Methodist Church share the same common priesthood. We have seen the concept of the ministry from two mainline churches; we now turn our attention to the priestly ministry among the African Indigenous Churches (AICs) with specific reference to Musama Disco Christo Church (MDCC)[162].

5.3.3. Priesthood/Ministry in Musama Disco Christo Church

The ordained ministry in the MDCC consists of pastors and prophets/prophetesses who are headed by the *Akaboha* who is regarded as a high priest. In essence, both the pastors and prophets/prophetesses function as priests who mediate between the lay people and the spiritual realm. The pastors and prophets/prophetesses offer priestly mediation for the entire congregation. In support of this view, Ekem asserts that "both ministries are in their own respects, committed to the task of representing the laity before God, and of being channels of divine revelation, whether through preaching, teaching, counselling, administration of the sacraments, or acts of effecting divine

---

[160] The Methodist Church Ghana. *The Constitution and Standing Orders of the Methodist Church Ghana*. 2000. S.O. 4 (1) & (4)
[161] The Methodist Church Ghana. *The Constitution and Standing Orders of the Methodist Church Ghana*. 2000. S.O. 4 (5)
[162] The other name for the MDCC is Army of the Cross of Christ Church.

healing in the physically and spiritually afflicted" [163] . For instance, the prophets/prophetesses are healers who mediate through prayer and fasting to bring healing to the lay who struggle with health. They are also involved in spiritual warfare against evil spirits on behalf of the members of the church and seek for direction and guidance from the spiritual realm. Ekem posits that the pastors are in charge of preaching, administering of baptism and the Lord's Supper, and the management of the local church[164].

In a personal interview with Feenakoma Charles Amissah-Arthur [165] on 28th November 2012 at the Elders Council Office in *Mazano*, he explained that God might call people into the MDCC ministry through various means such as dreams, visions and even sicknesses. Those who are called through sicknesses are mostly struck by illnesses and are healed on their visit to the church. After healing, it is then revealed to them that they are being called to be priests of the MDCC; and until they opt for the priesthood, the illness would be revisited on them. According to Amissah-Arthur in the same interview, elderly persons in the church guide those who feel called to discern properly into their call. The moral characters of those who feel called are taken into consideration to determine how genuine the call may be. Candidates for the ministry are offered priestly training and practices of the church at *Mazano* and afterwards taken to Good News Theological College in Accra for theological studies.

Ekem affirming what is said above also stressed that candidates for both the offices of the pastor and prophet/prophetess undergo training at *Mazano,* which may last for six months to two years or more depending on the candidate's previous qualifications[166]. Ordination into the pastoral and prophetic offices is in two stages in the sense that candidates who passed out from training are put on probation for a period and depending on their performances, they are finally ordained into their respective offices by the *Akaboha* at *Mazano*. It is also the sole prerogative of the *Akaboha* to promote them to higher ranks in the ministry when he deems it fit.

Baeta acknowledges the existence of a "Holy Place" in which there is the "Holy of Holies" at *Mazano* and the *Akaboha* as the "High Priest" enters into the sacred place during consecration and ordination of prophets/prophetesses and pastors/priests to pray on their behalf (ordinands for the ministry). Baeta again alleges that the *Akaboha* is also the only minister of the church who is bestowed with the mandate to enter into the "Holy of Holies" to pray on behalf of the whole church at any time of

---

[163] Ekem, JDK. 2009. Pg 129
[164] Ekem, JDK. 2009. Pg 125
[165] He has been a priest for twenty-eight years and the administrative officer of MDCC as at 28th November 2012.
[166] Ekem, JDK. 2009. Pg 125

his choice[167]. Ekem also explicates that as the "Highest Spiritual Head of the Church"; the *Akaboha* enters into the "Holy Place" and performs the annual rite of marking their holy objects "with the blood of an unblemished ram". He also anoints "the foreheads of participants as well as the doors of the representative houses in a way similar to ancient Israel's Passover ritual in Egypt"[168]. It seems that, the activities of the *Akaboha* at the "Holy of Holies" such as offering prayers on behalf of the church is an allusion to a Jewish practice in which the priest on duty goes into the Holy of Holies in the Temple to pray on behalf of the people (Lk 1:5-8). It also supports the view that the *Akaboha* is not just a priest in word but in essence and endowed with all sacerdotal functions within the Musama Disco Christo ecclesial context.

5.5. Conclusion

The discussion focused on the parallels of the Catholic Priesthood in the African Traditional Religion, Presbyterian Church, Methodist Church and Musama Disco Christo Church. We observed that the African traditional priests are mediators between the deity and the adherents of the religion while the Presbyterian and Methodist ministers are representative priests who do not function in any way as mediators. It was also discussed that the ministers in Mussama Disco Christo Church are priests who function as mediators between God and their congregation. The spiritual head of the church (the *Akaboha*) is bestowed with authority to perform all sacerdotal functions in the context of the Mussama Disco Christo Church.

---

[167] Baeta, C.G., 1962. Pg 45
[168] Ekem, JDK. 2009. Pg 128

CHAPTER VI

CONCLUSION

5.0. Conclusion

The book has been on the distinctiveness of the Catholic priesthood in the face religious pluralism in Ghana. The Catholic priesthood is a divinely initiated call to which one answers by going through seminary formation, accepting ordination and participating in the priesthood of Jesus Christ through the ministry of the Church. By ordination, the priest is no longer a man of his own as he becomes *alter Christus* and acts in *persona Christi* and he is ordained for the people of God. The Catholic priest is a man of service who ought to serve in whatever capacity the Church places him.

Furthermore, the priest is a man of distinction by virtue of the Sacrament of Ordination by which he is set apart to perform sacerdotal functions such as presiding over the celebration of the Eucharist, which is a re-enactment of the Christ's sacrifice at Calvary in a bloodless manner. For the priest, the mandate to do so was handed over to him at his ordination and it was the same mandate that Christ handed over to the apostles at the Last Supper. For the Catholic priest, he shares in the priesthood of Christ and plays the triple functions of Christ namely- a priest, prophet and king. The identity and authority of the Catholic priest resides in Jesus Christ the High Priest.

Although the study focused on the Catholic priesthood, it also narrowly included the notion of priesthood within the African Traditional Religions with emphasis on the Akan concept, and the parallels of the Catholic priesthood in the Presbyterian and Methodist Churches as Protestant traditions and the Musama Disco Christo Church (MDCC) as an African Indigenous Church.

The parallel of the Catholic priesthood within the Protestant Churches is the ordained ministry. Members of the ordained ministry within the Protestant Churches are referred to as reverend ministers or pastors. They may be referred to as priests but not in the context of Catholic tradition. Such Protestant priests only act as "representative priests" but are not priests in the essence of the term and do not have any exclusive sacerdotal functions. Meanwhile the MDCC recognizes the existence of a priestly ministry reserved for those ordained in the church. For the MDCC, such priests are not just "representatives" but priests in essence who possess sacerdotal rights within the context of the MDCC.

6.1. Recommendations

From the study, it has been noted that Catholic priests are to serve in whatever capacity the Church places them. In their service, they serve the people of God, the Church, for whom they are ordained. For that matter, priests must make themselves available, approachable and accessible to the people of God. Priests should draw closer and carry themselves in a way that would make the people of God open up to them for assistance for the salvation of their souls. In doing so, the congregation should also not take priests for granted but give them the full respect and support that their sacred office deserves.

Furthermore, the views of some priests revealed that the most difficult and common challenge for all priests is the promise/vow of obedience. It is our recommendation that all parish priests and priests occupying hierarchical positions to deal with assistant priests with much love and not to lord over them. They should enter into fraternal dialogue with assistant priests on issues rather than making it appear to be a command for them to obey without complaint. Parish priests and priests in other superior positions should promote and maintain filial relationship with assistant priests as the Fathers of the Second Vatican Council admonished.

Again, the study revealed that some relatives put undue pressure on priests for financial support, making the vow of poverty difficult for such priests. We recommend intensive education for the laity to know that priests in Africa are not monthly salary earners and for that matter may not be in the position to provide constant financial support. For this reason, relatives of priests should desist from seeing them as their source of revenue. Nevertheless, the Church should also consider increasing stipends given to her priests in order for them to be able to assist their relatives financially when the need arises. In Ghana and specifically with the Akans, males are obliged customarily to contribute financially in the upbringing of their nephews and nieces. The Akan Catholic priest, who simply has just enough to survive, finds it difficult in fulfilling his customary obligation towards his nephews and nieces.

In addition, we observe from the study that some Catholic laity holds the erroneous view that the church is a clerical society. There is the need to emphasize in catechism that the Church is not clerical but hierarchical. The laity should be made to know that the Church is a family of God, in which both the clergy and the laity have their respective responsibilities and roles without confusion. The lay members ought to identify themselves as true members of the Church which is the family of God, and also assume more active roles in this sacred family.

In brief, the entire study has elucidated the concept of the Catholic priesthood and has clearly shown how distinct the Catholic priesthood is from the ordained ministry within the Protestant tradition and other forms of priesthood in a religio-pluralistic society like Ghana. The distinction lies in the fact that the Catholic priesthood is a priestly ministry in the essence of the term, and realistically Catholic priests are mediating servants who offer sacrifice. They are *alter Christus* and acts *in persona Christi* when offering priestly duties such as administering the Sacraments. However when the same term is applied to Protestant ordained ministers, it is only used in the metaphorical sense, thus they are "representative priests". Consequently, they are not priests in the real sense of the word. Also, when the same priestly term is used in the indigenous religion (African Traditional Religion), it is meant in the realistic sense of the term but has nothing to do with Jesus Christ.

BIBLIOGRAPHY

Achtemeier, P.J. (Gen. Ed.). *Harper's Bible Dictionary*. Bangalore: Theological Publications, 1990.

Agbeti, J.W., 1986. *West African Church History: Christian Missions and Church Foundations 1482-1919*. Leiden: E.J. Brill.

Baeta, C.G. *Prophetism in Ghana*. London: SCM Press Ltd, 1962.

Bourke, M.M. "The epistle to the Hebrews". in: *The New Jerome Biblical Commentary*. London: Burns and Oates, 1995.

Brown, R.E. *Priest and Bishop: biblical reflections*. New York: Paulist Press, 1970.

Burge, G.M. "Deacon, Deaconess". in: *Evangelical Dictionary of Theology*, 2nd ed. Michigan: Baker Academic, 2001.

Burrghardt, W.J. "What is a Priest?" in: *The Sacraments: Readings in Contemporary Sacramental Theology*. New York: Alba House, 1981.

Cape Coast Archdiocese, 2003. *Landmarks in the history of the Catholic Church in the Archdiocese of Cape Coast, Ghana*. In: Program brochure for the Reception and Thanksgiving Mass of H.E. Peter Cardinal Kodwo Appiah Turkson.

Dunn, P.J. *Priesthood: a re-examination of the Roman Catholic theology of the Presbyterate*. New York: Alba House, 1990.

Ekem, J.D.K. *Priesthood in Context: A study of Priesthood in some Christian and Primal Communities of Ghana and its Relevance for Mother-Tongue Biblical Interpretation*. Accra: SonLife Press, 2009.

Ekwunife, A.N.O. The Priesthood in African Traditional Religion. *Bigard Theological Studies*, 19 (1), 5-39 pp, 1999.

Eliade, M. (Gen. Ed). *The Encyclopedia of Religion*. Vol. II, New York: Macmillan Publishing Company, 1987.

Encyclopaedia Judaica. Jerusalem: Keter Publishing House Jerusalem Ltd, 1972.

Gleeson, B. Ordained Persons and their Ministries: New Testament Foundations and Variations. *Australian eJournal of Theology*, 7, 1-13 pp, 2006.

Hahn, S. *Many are Called: Rediscovering the Glory of the Priesthood*. New York: Doubleday, 2010.

Halligan, N. *The Sacraments and their Celebration*. New York: Society of St. Paul, 1986.

Kloppenburg, B. *The Ecclesiology of Vatican II*. Chicago: Franciscan Herald Press, 1974.

Korsah, L.A. Towards an Understanding of Priesthood in the Realistic Sense from the Perspective of New Testament Theology. *Journal of Religion and Theology* Vol. 4 (2), pp. 6-9, 2020. ISSN 2637-5907.

Korsah, L.A. & Appiah-Kubi, F. Towards an Understanding of Ministerial Priesthood in the light of Priesthood of the Baptized. *Asian Horizons, Dharmaram Journal of Theology, 9(2)* pp 310-323, 2015.

Macquarrie, J. *Principles of Christian Theology*. 2nd ed. New York: Charles Scribner's Sons, 1977.

Martos, J. *Doors to the Sacred: A Historical Introduction to the Sacraments in the Catholic Church*. New York: Image Books, 1982.

Mbiti, J.S. *African Religions & Philosophy*. London: Heinemann, 1969.

McCauley, G. "The Priest: A Simple Reminder". in: *The Sacraments: Readings in Contemporary Sacramental Theology*. New York: Alba House, 1981.

McFarlan, D.M. *Dictionary of the Bible*. New Lanark: Geddes & Grosset, 2003.

McKenzie, J.L. *Dictionary of the Bible*. London: Cassell Publishers Limited, 1968.

Microsoft, "Ghana". In: *Microsoft Student 2009 [DVD]*. Redmond, WA: Microsoft Corporation, 2008.

Mitchell, N. *Mission and Ministry: History and Theology in the Sacrament of Order*. Wilmington, Delaware: Michael Glazier, 1982.

O'Malley, W.J. *Sacraments: Rites of Passage*. Chicago: Thomas Moore, 1995.

Opoku, K.A. *West African Traditional Religion*. Accra: FEP International Private Limited, 1978.

Perrin, J.M. *The Minister of Christ*. Dublin: M.H. Gill & Son Ltd, 1964.

Powell M.A. *Introducing the New Testament: A Historical, Literary and Theological Survey*. Michigan: Baker Academic, 2009.

Power, D.N. "Order". in: *Systematic Theology: Roman Catholic Perspectives*. Vol. II. Minneapolis: Fortress Press, 1991.

Quarcoopome, T.N.O. *West African Traditional Religion*. Ibadan: African Universities Press, 1987.

Samwini, N.I., 2006. *The Muslim Resurgence in Ghana since 1950 and its Effect upon Muslims and Muslim-Christian Relations*. Berlin: LIT Verlag.

Schmaus, M. Dogma 5: *The Church as Sacrament*. London: Sheed and Ward Inc, 1975.

Toon, P. "Bishop". in: *Evangelical Dictionary of Theology*, 2nd ed. Michigan: Baker Academic, 2001.

Trouve M.L., (Gen. Ed.). *The Sixteen Documents of Vatican II (Introductions by Douglas G. Bushman)*. Boston: Pauline Books & Media, 1999.

Wallace, R.S. "Elder". In: *Evangelical Dictionary of Theology*, 2nd ed. Michigan: Baker Academic, 2001.

Wood, D.R.W. (Gen. Ed.). *New Bible Dictionary*. 3rd Ed. Nottingham: Inter-Varsity Press, 1996.

Internet Sources:

2009. *Mussama Church: History of MDCC* [online] (2009) available at: http://mdccgh.blogspot.com [assessed on July 13, 2012]

Hardon, J.A., 1998. *The Priesthood* [online] (2000) available at: http://www.realpresence.org [accessed in March 2011].

Korsah, L.A. & Oku, G. K. Christian Ministerial Priesthood: a biblical survey on Catholic Priesthood. *E-Journal of Religious and Theological Studies*, September 2019 Issue, Volume 1 Number 3, ISSN 2458–7338, pp 19–25, DOI: https://doi.org/10.32051/09301902.

Korsah, L.A. The specificity of Catholic Priesthood in a Religio-Pluralistic Society: the Ghanaian case. *E-Journal of Religious and Theological Studies*, February 2019 Issue, Volume 1, Number 1, ISSN 2458 – 7338, pp. 169-179, DOI: https://doi.org/10.32051/02211914.

Mathew, P.G., 1996. *The Priesthood of All Believers* [on line] (1996) available at: http://members.dcn.org [accessed in March 2011].

Ratzinger, J., 1990. *On the Nature of the Priesthood* [online] (1990) available at: http://CatholicCulture.org [accessed on 24th April 2013].

Unpublished Work

Yim, Cherlsoon. 2004. *Understanding Islam, its history in Ghana, and an effective evangelistic strategy to overcome Islamic influence in Ghana.* Doctor of Ministry thesis submitted to Liberty Baptist Theological Seminary. Lynchberg, Virginia.

Oral Source involving interview:

Interview with Rev Feenakoma Charles Amissah-Arthur, Pastor and Administrative Officer of MDCC, at the Elders Council Office at Mazano on 28th November